CW01666351

LITTLE HAVEN

IN THE

WOODS

Follow your dreams

Louise

LITTLE HAVEN IN THE WOODS

LOUISE GREEN

Copyright © 2023 by Louise Green

All rights reserved.

ISBN:978-1-7380844-0-1

This is a work of creative nonfiction. The events are portrayed to the best of Louise Green's memory. While all the stories in this book are true, some names and identifying details have been changed to protect the privacy of the people involved.

For my Gran,
Every day your love, strength and courage inspired me to never stop pursuing my dreams
Thank you for being you

Contents

Foreword

"Why do you want to buy a piece of land?" I got asked this a lot and I often ask myself the same question.

It's not that I don't know the answer, but more so that there is no simple answer that captures the truth.

I desired a place of our own, with abundant space and unrestricted views. Freedom to choose who and what would be there. To have a garden that could expand, trees that could grow without restriction, trails, and paths, and unique outdoor spaces. Fewer boundaries and rules, a place of opportunity and potential. Freedom to wander, be quiet and breathe.

There have been so many unique, challenging, uncomfortable, and exhilarating moments in this adventure. This is my record of them. To remember the ups and downs and share them with you. Our story of finding our little haven in the woods and what we did with it. I hope it will inspire and encourage you. Your determination, tenacity, and perseverance dictate success, not external resources and knowledge.

Dave, my husband, and I were starting from very different perspectives. This project has taught us a lot about each other and ourselves. We sometimes went wrong, were lucky, made bad choices, were naïve, worked hard, and also made good choices. This is a story about raw land, our challenges in developing and building there, and what's possible.

We found our place. We are very happy with what we achieved, what we built, and how it turned out. Is it perfect? Yes, and no. There's always something to strive for, even when we love it. We achieved everything we wanted, but not in the ways we imagined we would. So jump in, read on, and let's go on our adventure!

PART ONE

Chapter One: Got What it Takes

One of my favourite quotes is *"You can never cross the ocean until you have the courage to lose sight of the shore"* by Christopher Columbus (or it may have been Andre Gide). This always inspires me! I interpret this as taking a leap of faith without knowing the outcome of achieving something worthwhile.

This is a story about frustration, challenges, and fear. Taking that leap. Dragging Dave along with me, and eventually achieving success, contentment, and living life with few regrets.

This isn't a how-to book. Many times we had very little clue what we were doing, with few resources beyond Google, YouTube, and our determination.

I hope our story will inspire and motivate you to define your own "haven in the woods" and keep striving until you reach it. If there is one thing you take away from reading our story, it is that with the right mindset, you can achieve whatever you desire.

There is no secret formula or magic bullet. It's about consistently taking action to get it. Be prepared to adapt, change direction, learn, and fail. How many times does a baby fall when learning to walk? Babies never give up because they can see everyone around them walking. They know it's possible, and they just keep trying until they can. It doesn't cross their mind to think their legs are not long enough, or I'm too young to walk, or no one is teaching me properly. They just keep trying.

Until the point where we started the search, the opportunities never seemed to be there. I didn't have the time; I wasn't with the right partner. There wasn't any land I could afford, and I always had a reason I couldn't have it.

I suppose I didn't want it enough to be prepared to change those things to make it happen. I didn't dare to jump into the unknown. This may be true of all the major changes we make. It is easy to blame other factors and create excuses for why we cannot have something. Yet if we look hard enough, there are always examples to prove exactly the opposite, success stories of people growing a business from nothing, survival stories against seemingly insurmountable odds, and many homesteaders who have their piece of land and living and building their dream. What made them successful? When others have failed. What did they have or do differently? They just kept trying and would not accept defeat. The only difference between success and failure is not giving up. Money, time, and intelligence are not the solution. By telling our story of how many mistakes we made and how much we didn't know, I hope to inspire you. If we can do this. It's possible for you to do this too.

I am constantly amazed when looking back at the series of events in my life that, at the time they occurred, they seemed random, unconnected, and just circumstantial. Years later, realizing if they had not happened in that order, it would be impossible to be doing what I am now. Is our whole life mapped out to follow a certain path that we have no real influence over? Is it luck or capitalizing on opportunities? Living in the moment with what you have around you.

Why is it so popular to want to escape from our daily lives? There are more and more TV shows, such as "Escape to the Country," "Build Off-Grid," and "Life Below Zero," with huge followings. Why do we love them so much? We are tired of the rat race, of working for the man. Everything gets more and more expensive. How can we simplify our lives? To allow us to focus on what's important. You hear it everywhere; we are all just so tired!

I started writing this about a year after the COVID-19 pandemic, which possibly sped up the trend. The pandemic allowed individuals to earn money without being limited to living nearby through remote work. COVID altered rules for many. It broke the system and sparked a search for a better way.

When I started thinking about where to begin writing this story, the real question became, '**When** did it all start?' What made us decide to start looking for a remote homestead? I no longer wanted to accept my excuses that I couldn't do it and started taking action toward achieving it.

Primarily in life, we are repeating tasks, thoughts, and actions that are familiar and habitual. There's a certainty and sense of comfort in the familiar. But if you want different results, you have to do different things.

We did research and tried to learn and anticipate the steps required for every stage, from the purchase of land to understanding the well. In every case, without exception, the challenges we expected for each task ended up being more straightforward and went smoothly. There were always more delays and frustrations in parts of the projects we thought would be simple. What have we learned from this? We learned that it's important to research and prepare thoroughly before starting a project, but also be ready to handle unexpected situations as they arise.

Chapter Two: Searching

Dave was studying the road map intently. "There's a gas station in Cherryville." I peered over his shoulder, looking at the map with doubt. "Well, I guess we haven't driven that way yet." I replied with resignation. I felt disheartened.

We had planned this three-day Easter getaway to British Columbia, Canada, as a fact-finding trip to look for a parcel of land to buy. After hours of pouring over the website "realtor.ca" at property listings, our search for a small acreage had gotten wider and further away from our primary choice of the Nakusp area. We had been actively looking for a property for about four months. We set our hearts on the Nakusp area after several summer camping trips. The area met our criteria: a long gardening season, lots of backcountry roads, hot summers, earlier spring, and within a day's drive from our current hometown of Canmore, Alberta. A 10-acre piece of land on Highway 6 caught our attention two weeks previously. I promptly emailed Nakusp realtor, Greg Hammond, expressing our interest and requested a property viewing. By the time he had gotten back to me, he said the land had multiple viewings, and someone was about to write an offer on it. There was also a run-down mobile home for sale in Edgewood, not exactly what we had in mind and undoubtedly outside of our budget, but I was keen to at least see something.

"Sorry, that too has multiple offers," he paused. "There's just not much around within your budget at the moment."

I could tell he didn't care at all. "We'll come out anyway. There may be something else available by the time we arrive", my optimism refusing to be quashed. The problem was that we were just too far away. He must have heard it a million times: people from out of the province looking to buy up any acreage, dream of building a cabin and escape. If we showed an intention by coming to stay in the area, maybe that would help, I reasoned internally. I was sure it would be worthwhile.

The slushy snow banks hadn't melted yet, but it amazed us at how warm it felt when we arrived. I jumped out of the truck into puddles. The warm moist pacific air felt like a gentle breath after the dry, harsh, chilly air of Canmore. We had chosen this B&B because it was the closest accommodation to the 10-acre parcel, which I had hoped would still be available. They advertised the Sunbeam retreat as an off-grid experience, with no electricity, no running water, and an outhouse for a bathroom. It was heaven! Geraldine had the wood burner roaring and candles lit when we arrived in the late afternoon dusk. It was so cozy, shadows dancing on the log walls, fire crackling, with large windows that looked out onto the surrounding forest. Just what I hoped we would have one day, a beautiful cabin on our land. She showed us the outhouse and outdoor shower, and gave us a tour of the wood-heated sauna.

The one-room cabin with wall-to-wall windows gave a sense of being surrounded by the forest. A bookcase filled with titles on yoga, finding your purpose, and living in gratitude It was the ideal place for a life transformation. A ladder provided access to the loft, which was equipped with a comfortable bed and fluffy down duvet, creating an ideal retreat to rest, relax and find purpose. The cabin, the sauna, the land surrounded by forest showed what was possible, but unfortunately, nothing was for sale. Or, more accurately, nothing within our budget that was for sale. If we had a few million to spend, then there were a lot more options. Even if we could have afforded that, it wasn't part of our goal, which was to buy something we could enjoy without needing to work 24-7 to pay for it.

My current level of dissatisfaction had nothing to do with where we were staying; it was so peaceful and calming. So here we were, staying in a beautiful B&B we found on Airbnb, with zero properties for sale to look at—no available internet connection to do any further research and intermittent cellphone service.

"OK, let's go then," I said. "We need gas for the drive home tomorrow, and I guess it will be good to explore that direction."

I held little hope of discovery. Highway 6 North headed up over the Monashee pass into Cherryville, Lumby, and onto Vernon. It was mostly crown land, and Cherryville was, even given my enthusiasm, just too far for us to realistically buy a property and travel to it regularly. Dave purposefully ignored my disappointment and kindly offered to drive. More often than not, I would have argued with him, but I didn't have the energy and slid into the passenger seat, dragging the map along and plugging in my dead cell phone. Some downsides to no electricity, I thought grumpily.

As we headed down the bumpy gravel road and back onto the highway, the sun peaked through the clouds, lightening my mood. Boy, it sure is pretty here. I couldn't help but feel lifted by the surroundings. The road bent sharply right and down, the vista opening up into the beautiful Inonoaklin Valley. I couldn't believe there were still piles of snow up by the B&B, yet here it felt like spring already. Green fields hugged the valley bottom, cows contentedly grazing in the warm sunshine.

We passed where we had judged the ten acres for sale to be on the left-hand side of the road. I looked longingly, hoping the deal might fall through. Ten acres was more than we wanted. What would we do with it all? I reasoned to myself to avoid disappointment. Dave hit the gas pedal as the road straightened out, and I glanced over at him, pondering the reason for the haste. I meant us to be looking for properties. We passed a small pull-in on the right with a stop sign. I glanced across and thought I saw a white sign hung in the tree set back from the road. It seemed oddly out of place. Was that a for sale sign? I was only half paying attention, and we had sped by before I could take notice.

We were soon going up and up, twisting and turning; the view over the guardrail led to giddy drop-offs to the rocks and the foaming river below. I got out the map to follow our progress as we wound our way up through the pass. Never a straight section, Dave was enjoying rally driving. I could imagine how it might be to drive in the winter and challenging for the snowplows to keep the road open.

"This is wild country," I said, looking across the valley and beyond. Nothing but trees, rock faces, and mountains stretching to the horizon—brilliant blue sky, a perfect backdrop for the acres and acres of forest.

Dave agreed. "There's not much in any direction from here. We are out in the middle of nowhere." The mountains, still capped with snow, differed greatly from those around

Canmore, lower and more rounded than angular. They seemed more accessible.

A sign announced we had reached the summit at 3900 ft, and we began the winding descent into Cherryville.

"The word Monashee is from the Gaelic *monadh*, meaning mountain, and *sith*, pronounced shee, meaning peace." Dave told me "Monashee, therefore, means mountain of peace." It always amazed me how much he knew about geography and places.

"It does feel peaceful here somehow," I said, enjoying being a passenger for a while, able to look around and appreciate the dramatic landscape. Given the twists and turns of the road, I was glad Dave was driving. I had shaken off my bad mood when we reached Cherryville and found our way to the gas station. We drove by a few appealing homesteads on the way into town and noticed one or two 'for sale' signs. Neither of us was sufficiently interested in their appearance to pursue more than a tertiary glance as we drove by. It was too far from our chosen target area.

When looking for houses and property, there are certain intangible criteria that we rely upon, not just about the actual land or house, but also about the area. The feeling you get when you experience a place that 'feels' good, and the right place for you. It is astonishing when making such a huge life changing purchase that many times it comes back to feeling that it is the right place and the right time.

"I'll drive back," I offered, "so you can enjoy the view." I had an idea to check out what I had thought was the sale sign I had seen on the way out, but did not want to seem foolish if it was nothing. We returned up and over the pass one more time, not knowing the road well; it was a challenging drive, hairpins left and right keeping me focused on the driving. I imagined having to drive this road every time I wanted to get to the city. That would be something very different to get used to, not having easy access to grocery stores, hardware stores, and supplies. Could we adapt to living here? Being self-sufficient, pre-planning, and being more organized would be necessary to live in a remote location. I thought it would be worth the inconvenience of the drive to have enough space and land to build a cabin and a garden as big as I wanted.

Back in the valley, as the road straightened out, I slowed, trying to remember where I had seen what I thought might be a sign.

Dave looked sideways at me. "What are you doing?"

"Well, I thought I saw something on the way out and just wanted to check it out." I was still reluctant to say what I was hoping to see.

"What was it?"

As he asked, there on the left, I saw it! A tattered for sale sign perched crookedly high in a birch tree.

Chapter Three: First Impressions

I casually pulled into the gravel road and stopped the truck. "Um, well, I thought I saw a sign." Pointing directly at the sign in the tree. "There it is." We looked at each other.

"I don't know" He was doubtful. "It looks pretty old," and I had to agree that the sign looked like it had been there for years.

"You're probably right, but I'm going to take a closer look" I couldn't read it properly. The faded orange FOR SALE sign had a handwritten telephone number. There was small writing below that I couldn't make out. I was curious about what they were selling. It might be just firewood or something.

The sign said five acres for sale with septic approval, water, and hydro. It was an Alberta phone number, which spurred me into action. This could be what we were looking for; maybe it was still for sale. But then again, no, it's probably old, perhaps sold like everything else around here. It's Easter Sunday, you can't call today. Perhaps no one will answer… Thoughts whirled back and forth in my mind. Do it, don't bother, do it!

"I'm going to call it," I stated deliberately. I looked at my phone, and amazingly, I had a cell signal at that spot. Mind made up, heart pounding, I dialled the number.

"Hello?" a female voice inquired. Oh, wow, someone answered. I could hardly believe it.

"Hi, this is Louise. I saw your for sale sign on the land in BC," I hesitated, not wanting to hear her say sorry it sold. "Is it still for sale?" I asked slowly.

"Why, yes, it is," she answered.

"Really?" I gave her another chance to confirm what I expected; it's sold. "Oh wow," now what? my mind raced… "We are right here by the sign now. Would it be OK if we take a look and walk around?" Conscious of us getting kicked off the Parson property we had looked at without permission before, I was keen to get permission this time.

"Yes, absolutely" She also gave us the price. She explained she knew little about it; she was selling it for her brother.

Dave was gesturing to me to put her on speakerphone so he could hear, but I was worried the call would drop the signal any moment, so I grimaced at him to be quiet. Then, wildly trying to quell the excitement and be as casual as I could, "OK then, we are interested. We will have a walk around and then give you a callback; thank you very much" We exchanged details and hung up.

I looked at Dave with difficulty, trying to stop the grin from splitting my face in two. I told him the price; he raised his eyebrows in disbelief.

"I know, right? That seems a reasonable price. She said we could have a walk around," I said, taking his hand. "Come on, let's go look."

There was a faint, overgrown trail disappearing around a curve into the trees. Several fallen, rotting birch trunks lay broken across the path. Last year's brown ferns drooped under a pine, spruce, and cedar canopy. A faint smell of mushrooms wafted up as our boots crushed the brown grass. The trees, left to their own devices, had become thick and crowded, ranging from 15 to 40 feet tall. Growing wherever they wanted—interspersed with white birch standing proudly tall between the evergreens. The terrain was level, with no sign of any fences or markers to designate the boundaries.

I looked at Dave and shrugged.

"Where shall we go? Follow this path, I suppose," I said to myself.

We were not sure if we were on the right land or not. We wandered slowly, following the indistinct trail, which disappeared around the bend away from the road. All we could hear was the drip of condensation from the trees; it was so still and so quiet. Several pockets of slushy snow still clung onto winter under the trees, but the ground was mainly bare and easy to walk.

We strolled, saying nothing, each lost in our thoughts. I turned around and walking backward, tried to gauge how far we had come; how big were five acres, anyway? I couldn't picture how big an area that was. After about 15 minutes of wandering, the trees thinned, and we came to a power line running perpendicular to our trail. There was a galvanized pipe sticking up out of the ground, covered with a white upturned bucket to our left.

Dave removed the bucket and peered down the pipe. "Do you think that's the well?"

"Could be." I did not know what a well might look like. I had visions of a round stone wall with a little wooden roof over it and a handle to wind the bucket up and down. My early life growing up in the UK, I had never seen a modern drilled well to know what it would look like.

He pointed up at the power lines overhead. "This must be where you'd get power for the land, too."

We could see a row of fence posts in the distance, and we guessed the edge of the property must be here somewhere. This area was quite different from the densely packed trees we had walked through at first. It was quite open ground with rocky, sandy soil, thin patches of grass, and shrubs growing wildly.

"What do you think?" I asked Dave cautiously. I was already in love with it, had put in an offer to buy, had built a cabin, and moved here in my imagination. Nevertheless, I was curious to know what Dave was thinking. He tends to be much less likely to give in to emotion and more logical in thinking.

None of this crazy idea to look for the land had been Dave's idea; how was he feeling now? It was not just pictured on a real estate website; we were there in person on land for sale. This was an actual place. Would the reality be too much?

To me, this place felt different, a much better prospect than anything we had looked at before. It would be much easier to build on, with no steep gradients to worry about, had a pleasant mixture of trees, and the ferns reminded me of woodlands growing in England.

He looked around, taking time to think about his answer. "It's flat, level ground, much better than those other places we looked at in Nakusp. The trees are smaller, too; that birch would make great firewood."

Well, he's not saying anything negative yet. This is a good sign, I thought. I could hardly stop myself from skipping back to the truck with excitement. My hands out stretched brushing the ferns and caressing the leaves as we headed back. We stumbled upon a clearing with a pile of logs stacked against a tree, and a circle of stones from an old campfire.

Dave went to look at the woodpile. "Someone must have camped here, but quite a while ago, it looks like."

"It makes a nice camp spot," I walked over to join him, looking around. "We could build a cozy cabin here."

It was far enough from the road to be private, and the trail seemed to end at the clearing. I glanced at Dave and wondered what he thought of my cabin suggestion. He nodded thoughtfully, which I took to be a good sign. I so wanted him to like it and see the possibilities.

"I think it's way better than anything we've seen before. The price is fantastic too. OK, it's got nothing on it yet, but there's a power line, a well, and good access to the road." All systems go as far as I was concerned. I could hardly contain my excitement.

Dave, with a rare burst of impulsiveness, jumped in. "Let's get some more details from Sarah and go from there. I don't think we can lose, based on the prices of others we've seen around here and the Nakusp area."

We were excited. It felt like we had finally found the perfect property that ticked all the boxes and had potential. We wanted to move quickly but feared the unknowns.

We already had the experience of the high demand for properties, but were also cognisant that this was a private sale. What did we need to do? Or need to find out? What if we were making a big mistake? We are both naturally adventurous people. But this was an enormous commitment together in a venture we were uncertain how to realize.

It filled our minds and conversation on the short ride back to the B&B. We phoned Sarah back to let her know we were extremely interested and wanted to see the deeds or any information she had on the lot boundaries, etc. We needed time to think, to allow ourselves to consider and explore the pros and cons. Dave lit the wood stove in the sauna. It was getting dark by the time it was hot enough, as we tiptoed in our towels down the short path in the chilly night air to the sauna. I collected snow to melt for steam.

The snow hissed as it hit the rocks heated on the stove, sending clouds of steam swirling in the small cedar room. As we sat in the glow of candlelight, cedar-scented steamy heat, the fire popped and crackled; we passed excited ideas back and forth. I was imagining what we could do there, growing a garden, having a cabin of our own, a sauna, an outdoor kitchen, so many ideas. Would we go for solar panels, or hook up to hydro? Did the well have water in it?

"So, are we going to go for it? Shall we put in an offer? As long as it looks good?" I felt we had already decided and wanted to get confirmation from Dave.

He nodded agreement. "Yes, I want to." This was it; an old for-sale sign had turned into a genuine opportunity. We were going for it. It felt as though life had taken a gigantic step in a new direction. We had a hard time sleeping because we were so excited.

Chapter Four: The Offer

Sarah had emailed us the only document she had on the property overnight. Sarah surprised me, as she didn't seem prepared with official documents for selling the land. It turned out it was quite a lot more complicated. The ownership of the land belonged to her deceased brother. Sarah had never visited it and knew nothing much about it. She was getting probate sorted out and assured us she had everything in place. She was warm, friendly, and thrilled we had called.

"You have made my day!" she said. We were en route to the ferry and only had a cell signal for a brief time. Not wanting to seem too eager, we left it that we would take a little more time to decide and get back to her. Now we had a huge dilemma. Should we speculate on a plot of land we had limited information about on the back of a brief walk around and short telephone call?

Neither of us had purchased property without a realtor before, and it felt very much outside our comfort zone. But given how difficult it was to find anything and the months we had been looking, did we want to pass up this potential opportunity? We were under pressure to act fast, so we made a gut decision. Not something we were that comfortable with, but we were more worried about losing out.

We needed professional advice. During the 7-hour drive home, we spoke to two lawyers, and they referred us three times to find someone local who could help us. We stuffed our heads full of knowledge about BC property law, land titles, probate, and grant of administration at every step. But we couldn't stop now; with our path chosen were determined to make this place ours.

We called Sarah, holding the phone between us on loudspeaker to make the offer. Dave and I hoping she had not already received another offer from someone else. We lowballed on our first offer, reasoning that we could always go higher. However, Sarah was firm on the price, and we could tell instantly by her voice that there would be no negotiation. With no hesitation, I looked at Dave, and he nodded, "OK, Sarah, fair enough. We will pay the full asking price. We have a lawyer and will write up a formal offer to you within the day."

It was done; we had found a place and made an offer that was verbally accepted. It just seemed so unreal, within two days, how different a position we were in. This was our biggest commitment made together, and that meant a lot to me, a solid foundation, security, and a dream hopefully about to come true.

But what a roller coaster, there were still so many unknowns, we had to get financing, we were unsure of the situation with probate, and the deeds for the land. Our lawyer said it could take three months because it is an estate sale. If all went well, we would be back on our land by the summer! I felt like this was all a dream.

As we had agreed price, Sarah and I opted to use the same lawyer for the sale. Sarah needed help with the administration of the estate; it all seemed straightforward. We emailed the signed offer to purchase to Sarah. Our lawyer was cautious about the timescale for completion, but hopefully, it would be ours within three months. Even with delays, we might have the last of the summer to get started.

With our knowledge of how hot the real estate market was, Dave and I were still nervous about getting a signed agreement from Sarah. Sealing the deal would allow us to relax a little. We seemed to be the only ones with any sense of urgency; it was frustrating. We wanted to move on and make plans but were so scared to tempt fate by assuming it was all going to work out. We felt vulnerable without a realtor, as there was no legal protection for the sale. Sarah, when we spoke to her, seemed genuinely nice, but we didn't know her or her circumstances at all. We were not sure how much we could trust the deal being completed.

Chapter Five: The Long Wait

A week later, still nothing back from Sarah… what was happening? How long did it take to sign the acceptance of the offer? I was panicking; what had happened? Did she have another offer? Had she changed her mind? Every worse scenario I could imagine had come true in my mind. A week felt like a month.

I was reluctant to keep phoning her every day. Maybe it was upsetting for her, but I eventually gave in and called. She had been having problems getting a witness for the acceptance, and her internet and cell service were spotty at home. They all seemed such normal reasons compared to the imaginary disasters my mind had created. What a relief! She was still keen to sell; so far it was still going to be ours.

Dave and I were also working on our financing and learning it would take more work to secure the money than we had expected. Although we had 50% of the purchase price in cash, banks were not in the habit of arranging traditional mortgages for raw land, with no house built on it. The acreage being in a different province also added extra complications. After a lot of discussions, meetings, and research, we chose a local credit union with less restrictive lending criteria.

We were looking at construction mortgages, loans, and traditional mortgages. The number of options and criteria to comply with was overwhelming. We had not dealt with borrowing for many years, and neither of us was familiar with the latest financing rules. We were unaware how limiting it was to only have the land as collateral, even with 50% of the purchase price down. Everything would pend on an appraisal of the land value.

Two weeks later, we finally received the signed acceptance of the offer back from Sarah. It had taken three weeks to get the approval. We felt relieved because we had a legally binding agreement, albeit pending getting our financing and completing probate.

We arranged the land appraisal with a local company, and yet again we were nervously waiting and relying on others, hoping feverishly for a favourable report. Never had I felt in such a vulnerable position where our dreams were in the hands of others. Trying to remain calm and realistic, hoping yet keeping everything in perspective. There would be other opportunities if this didn't pan out, it would be because there was a better opportunity waiting. Everything happens for a reason. I kept promising myself.

We had already dealt with a similar situation just a few months previously. For a few months in November of the year before (Nov 2020), I had been scanning the Realtor website and propertyguys.com, looking for small parcels of land or run-down cabins for sale. Since my divorce and sale of the family home many years before, I felt insecure owning no property and seeing prices constantly rising; I wanted to invest the money I had and create some security. Dave and I had been together for several years, and while he owned his own home, which we lived in, it wasn't the same as if we owned something together. I hoped for us to have a joint investment not just as an asset but as a shared dream and something we could build and have together.

Few properties were available, and the pandemic made it difficult to travel and make appointments to see anything. I had spotted a cute-looking place near Parson, BC. It was two acres with an old run-down cabin. One Sunday in late November, we headed that way for a drive and take a look. We pulled up and plodded through the snow to the ramshackle building. I cupped my hands to peer in through the dirty windows and saw somebody had left in a hurry. There was garbage littered across the floor and beer cans on the kitchen counter. But my mind was already seeing how we could clean it up. A large willow tree at the front shaded the porch, with a sweeping meadow gently sloping toward the road. The Bugaboo mountain range framed views across the Columbia River wetlands in the distance. The only thing I tried not to notice was the road noise; I didn't want to acknowledge any negatives.

Dave was quiet during our walk around. Even when prompted, he wasn't keen to give much comment. Which I knew was a sign he wasn't that enamoured with the place. I was a little disappointed myself as I wanted to fall in love with it and have that 'feeling' that it was the right place. It just didn't feel that way, however much I wanted it to.

A few weeks later, we were still talking about it. I was online with my family in the UK and looked up the listing to send them a link so they could look at it. After several minutes, I gave up; I just couldn't seem to find it. The listing was gone; it had either sold or been taken off the market. Initially, I felt disappointed because although we had taken no active steps to buy it immediately; I had planned to revisit it in the future. As it hadn't been completely perfect, it wasn't too big a deal to let go of it. So, we went back to searching.

The land near Edgewood was what we had been waiting for and would be a far different story if we lost out on it now. It already felt like we had much more time and energy invested in securing it.

Chapter Six: Now What?

A week after the appraiser visited the land, we received a copy of the appraisal; it was good news. To get financing approval, we needed to match or exceed the offer price, but it was great to find out that the land was appraised for a higher value than our sale price. Not by a huge amount, but enough to solidify our decision.

At the beginning of May, we heard from Sarah that, unfortunately; she was still slogging through the probate estate situation, and the documents needed to be resealed in the BC courts. Given the pandemic and many public buildings closed, the backlog of cases would mean more delays.

By June, we could waive the finance condition, so now we had everything in place from our side. But we had missed the deadline to waive our conditions on the finance. It was worrisome that we were out of contract and Sarah could accept another offer. After all, the sale sign was still up in the tree. Maybe someone else would call her with a better higher offer.

Another month had gone by, and yet again, I had a tough time getting hold of Sarah, and I felt for sure she was avoiding us because she had found another buyer. Why hadn't we taken down the for sale sign when we were there before? Maybe we could go out there again and remove it. Thoughts plagued my sleepless nights.

We asked to amend the contract and extend the close date to keep everything legitimate and help with our stress levels. With the amended contract sent, if Sarah could just sign and get it back to us, we could feel more relaxed that we had a legal contract again.

We had been confident in our credit scores and financial stability when we started looking for land. Certain we could borrow as much as we needed for whatever dream property we could find. However, the reality was more sobering and forced us to have some hard conversations. We had used all our cash plus borrowed money to buy the land, which left us wondering what we would do next.

I had made it a long-term goal of mine to own some property for security in the future. But I did not want to be obligated to a large mortgage payment that would force me to work all the time in order to afford it and never have time off to enjoy it. With no buildings or facilities, what would we do with the land once we finally owned it? If we eventually built a home there, how would we afford it? If we were to borrow more money, could we get approval for increased borrowing? It seemed unlikely. Even if we borrowed more, the repayments would be so high that we'd never be able to take time off work to go there. I much preferred the idea of developing what we could over several years without borrowing and paying for things as we saved, doing most of the work ourselves. Dave strongly opposed the suggestion, arguing that we lacked the knowledge to do the work ourselves. That we would not have enough money to buy materials, and it would be far better to get more long-term finance for any home building.

We went back and forth; I hated the idea of borrowing and wanted to do the work ourselves, and he didn't want to do the work and wanted to pay someone else. Neither of us was right or wrong. We just had very different ideas. It was a moot point, as we didn't even own the land yet.

We had the trailer, and that would have to suffice for now. Staying in the trailer would give us time to work out what to do, pending the eventual purchase.

Given the slow pace of the purchase, it hadn't slowed my enthusiasm in planning what would happen next once we finalized the sale.

I am often in awe of circumstances that are revealed to you months or years after the original event happens. We were 'persuaded' to buy a travel trailer in January, six months previously, long before we had even heard of the Inonoaklin Valley. This had arisen because of a family member of mine (Jason) being thrown into taking early retirement. He had not planned this and wanted to sell his travel trailer to downsize. Dave and I were (and still are) avid tent campers, so we had never really considered getting a trailer.

We were happy with our tent, had all the gear, and felt having a trailer was kind of cheating and not 'true' camping! Jason was persuasive and in need of help, so we relented. Given our initial reluctance, we ended up admitting there were benefits to extending our camping season with the trailer. It was quite luxurious having a fridge, microwave, toilet, and shower!

Fast forward to our potential land purchase, and having the trailer now became a key part of our planning. We hoped to stay in the travel trailer on the land during the summer. While we worked on agreeing on a more permanent accommodation solution.

In our previous visits to the area, we had noticed some odd structures. At first, we had thought they were just poor construction or lazy builders, but then we learned better. Many trailers had either a steep roofed pole barn built around the trailer or a frame on top of the trailer, giving the usually flat-topped trailer a peaked roof. Two words–snow load! These strange-looking structures had an important function. They kept the heavy wet snow off the roof. They can get up to 11 feet of snow in the valley. Building code requires roofs to be designed to carry 95 lbs per square foot. I was concerned about leaving the trailer for several months without visiting over the winter, with no protection against heavy snow. It was essential for us to build some type of structure to protect the trailer.

Back to the internet and our friend Google. As usual, once you start searching for things, as if by magic, Google comes up with useful suggestions. That can be helpful; at this point it seemed opportune (perhaps later, we would change our mind–hindsight is a wonderful thing). We started researching storage sheds and buildings. Well, perhaps I should say I started researching. Dave was preaching patience and waiting until we owned the land. Wise man. "Anyway, fortune favours the brave," I thought. We chose a Quonset-style steel building kit because of our inexperience in building and construction. This would be ideal to overwinter the trailer and later function as a workshop/garage. With complete installation instructions, it seemed like it would be simple to put up. Just like a big Meccano set, I thought. The company had a sale on a "make us an offer" deal. I made an offer, and we got a great deal on a steel building that would certainly hold up to the snow load and be big enough to store our trailer. The delivery date was for approximately August, which seemed ideal given the timeline to complete the buying of the acreage, which we hoped would be soon. We had made our first big purchase and had a place to keep our trailer secure over the winter. All we now needed was the land to build it on.

Chapter Seven: No Progress

Another three weeks, and still no amendment signed by Sarah. Stress levels rose again; it felt like a true roller coaster. Then unexpectedly, we got an email, saying that she didn't know what was happening, and the lawyer seemed to keep asking for the same documents. For us, at least it meant she was still wanting to sell us the property and gave us some peace of mind. Dave and I are literal people and feel much better having the paperwork in order.

But, the pressing matter of the steel building we had ordered, the delivery date, was now causing us to worry. We were in the middle of June already; what if we hadn't closed the deal by the time it was due to be delivered? Could we delay delivery, or find somewhere else to store it? Perhaps it had not been such a good idea to buy at the point I did. It had been an impulse buy in some respects.

The months were ticking by faster than we would have liked. We had hoped, even though unrealistic, that we might get some of the summer on the property. Unfortunately, that was rapidly fading away. We had no inkling at that time if we would ever own it.

Summer in BC raised another issue that we had previously not paid much attention to: forest fires. Apart from the nuisance and annoyance of smoke shrouding the mountains and clogging our lungs for weeks at a time. This year it was to play a much larger role, just as we seemed to be closer to completing the sale. In addition, a couple of wildfires were being watched in the locality of our land.

Fairly typical for lightning strikes to start wildfires, especially in recent years, but we had never had so much of a personal stake before. The fires were growing and suddenly out of control, but still far away from the land. I had reached out to some friends in the area, and they didn't seem too concerned at that point. Yet as the days of waiting for progress on the land sale ticked by, the fires grew and were steadily getting closer to the land. We stayed in touch on Facebook and watched with horror as the inferno swallowed up cabins and homesteads.

Embers falling, everyone pitching in to hose down and patrol for hot spots. Surely BC fire crews would be there soon. But there were so many wildfires in BC that there just wasn't enough capacity to deal with every fire burning. Priority had to go to those closest to communities. They issued voluntary evacuation orders, which seemed unnecessary, as the fires were still quite distant. But then we realized it wasn't so much the proximity to the land, but that escape routes and roads were affected and hampering fire fighting efforts.

Then it became a mandatory evacuation, including the area surrounding "our" land, as we felt it was. Even if we had officially bought the land, we would not have been able to get there now because of the road and area closures. We feared the fire would leave nothing except ashes when we could travel there. We knew our worries were small compared to others, yet we still watched the wildfire maps and monitored the Facebook community. What a community it was, organizing, pulling together, and showing the world what a small village can do. It made us even more determined to become part of it.

Meanwhile, we could only wait to hope for the, so far, elusive closing date. Would we still want the land if it was nothing but bare earth? If all the trees were gone? We thought so, but it was not something we could even contemplate. Trees will regrow.

Later that month, Sarah asked the lawyer for an update on the resealing; this was encouraging and gave us hope she was now picking up the pressure on the lawyer. But then, as we were becoming used to one step forward and two backward, we found out they were still waiting on documents from the Alberta courts. How long was that going to take? Almost the next day, the credit union that was financing our purchase told us that the close date would be the end of August. And that we might need to reapply for financing as the mortgage application had expired. We found this out from the credit union and not our lawyer. It was looking increasingly like it would never happen, and now what would we do about the building delivery?

We had heard nothing from the steel building company yet, so we hoped that there would be delays on that too. A later delivery would give us a chance to finalize the purchase of the land first.

After much waiting, emails and phone calls, the lawyer had documents ready for Sarah to sign and the process advanced.

At the beginning of August, I decided to ask Sarah if we could store the building on the land, even though the purchase was not complete. If she agreed, it would save us from worrying about the delivery. In the meantime, of us dealing with courts and lawyers, there was some good news about the wildfire situation. People could finally return to their homes; the evacuation order was over. The fire was still burning but being held by the fire breaks.

Chapter Eight: Taking Another Look

We knew we would have to be on-site to take delivery of the steel building if Sarah would allow us to store it on the land ahead of the purchase completion. We asked Sarah if we could camp on the land when the steel building arrived, so we could pay the driver and decide where to store it. None of that would be possible without being there. The next challenge was already on our mind. The building weighed 2400lbs and was on a pallet; how were we going to get it off the delivery truck? With no equipment or local knowledge.

On August 18, they notified us they would load the steel building on August 25. But we still needed consent from Sarah to store the building there. It was getting very tense. It felt like we were slowly being crushed between progress and needing agreement. Yet again, our close date had lapsed, and we were out of contract! With more at stake than ever, there was still no word from the BC courts to indicate they had accepted the documents. At last, the lawyer got hold of Sarah, and she gave verbal consent we could stay on the land and store the steel building. We quickly made a plan to drive out with our trailer, stopping in Nakusp to sign documents and pay the balance for the purchase.

On August 24, we were on our way; the trailer hitched up, heading towards Golden. The sun was shining, and it was a beautiful fall day. It was with mixed feelings; we were almost at our goal, and it felt like it was so close to happening, yet it was still not ours yet. We were cognisant of being respectful and not taking advantage that we must just stay there making no changes, as it wasn't ours yet.

While on our way toward Rogers Pass from Golden, we received a call from the trucking company to confirm delivery arrangements. "Yes, we have everything organized for receiving the delivery and have the bank draft" I was excited to let them know we were ready.

"So, the truck should arrive with you on September 3rd," the delivery company confirmed. I looked at Dave, confused; it was only August 24th.

"September 3rd? We thought it was being delivered tomorrow." I was confused. How did we get the dates so wrong?

"We loaded it on the truck in Ontario on August 24, and it takes about 5-6 days to get to you," she explained patiently.

"Oh" feeling very stupid, I realized my mistake. In my excitement, I had heard "being delivered" on August 25, not loaded in Ontario. So unless our truck driver has wings, we would be very early!

"OK, thank you. So it will arrive on September 3rd?" I wanted to be sure we had the correct date.

"What do we do now?" I turned to Dave. We were now driving to receive a building that wasn't arriving for another six days. We couldn't afford to stay that long and be away from work commitments. Thinking rapidly, ever conscious we were driving further away with every minute, we had to make a quick decision. Carry on or turn back? We tossed the options back and forth for a few minutes. It was so disappointing to think we would not be going to the land and the workshop would not be arriving as we expected. But if we carried on, we would run out of time and have to return home before they delivered the workshop.

I switched on the indicator, and we turned off the highway, completing a U-turn. We didn't have enough time to reflect on what had happened before we headed home. One minute we are excitedly driving to see what we hope is our new land. The next heading home, feeling stupid for getting the delivery wrong. Perhaps it was an omen and sent to teach us a valuable lesson. Do not assume things will turn out right. Silence filled the truck as we wound our way back through the Kicking Horse Pass out of Golden. This was a very different outcome from how this day was supposed to have turned out.

My mind racing, always looking for solutions, as we passed Field, I really, really did not want to go home like this.

"Let's spend the night at Takkakaw Falls Campground," I said. "It just seems too disappointing to go directly home. Let's spend the night there and then head home tomorrow."

"OK, good idea," Dave said. Just in time, as we got close to the turnoff for the campground. We needed some time to process what had happened and the change in direction. My mistake highlighted how absolutely sure of arrangements we needed to be. This was not just a small project, but had lots of moving parts, people, and organization. It was scary to think we could have got there and not realized the mistake. Were we ready to take on this project if we could get this simple part wrong?

It turned out to be a blessing that we did not get all the way there. After setting up the trailer at the campground, we discovered we were out of propane. We had only just filled the two tanks, so we knew something was wrong for this to happen. One pigtail (the hose connecting the propane tank to the trailer) was old and had perished, causing a leak. So, with hindsight, it worked out after all. If we had travelled to Edgewood and discovered we had no propane and needed to repair the pigtail, it would have been impossible to stay there. After all, we needed propane to run the fridge, heat water, and cook. For our one-night camping, we managed by just drinking beer, but an entire week in Edgewood would have been more challenging.

Chapter Nine: Finally on Our Way

On September 1st, we set off again with our trailer in tow for our second endeavour to visit the land. We had rearranged our meeting with the lawyer in Nakusp to sign the mortgage and purchase documents. So much was unknown, and we still had no idea how long probate and the courts would take. But it seemed more likely, and the fear of not getting to buy the land was gradually fading.

Being replaced by the new challenges regarding the steel workshop and building in an unknown, relatively remote area. If we needed something, Canadian Tire was an hour and a half away, not just around the corner as we were used to. To prepare for the trip, I had been writing so many lists to ensure we had everything we would need.

We had recently purchased a solar panel and a new battery for the trailer. "boondocking" was an unknown term and an unfamiliar experience for us. I had come across the word boondocking in my research; it means to camp in an RV or trailer with no access to water, sewer, or electrical hookups. Would the trailer fridge work on propane? How would we get the steel building pallet off the truck? How long would the battery power last? Would the solar panel give us enough charge?

We were growing excited despite the unknowns. With the realization that we were actually on our way to what we hoped would end up being our land. It was six months since we had been there, and summer was almost over. Would it still look as we remembered it? The ferns that had been brown and dead over the winter, would they still be green or had already started browning again? Would the trail we followed on our first trip have become overgrown?

The journey felt like it was taking forever. We wanted to measure and mark out the boundaries of the five acres, as there were no fences or markers at all that we remembered. So, we could have a sense of how big the area was and start thinking about where we would build our cabin and gardens. We didn't know if we had any neighbours or how they may feel about having new people close by.

After a brief stop in Nakusp, we had everything signed and sealed and were on the last leg. The trip from Canmore to the land takes about six hours of driving. It's 500km, goes over Rogers Pass, requires us to take two ferries, and change time zones. However, it is a beautiful drive and never gets dull; the mountains are always changing and look stunning at all times of the year.

It was mid-afternoon as we rolled off the Needles ferry, calm and sunny, lower Arrow Lake smooth as a mirror, reflecting the brilliant blue sky. The road winds up over the low mountain range flanking the lake and then drops steeply into the Inonoaklin Valley. The road then straightens out across green fields, and there it was, the little turnout on the right. We pulled up on the gravel.

Chapter Ten: The Land

We took in the view, while sitting in the truck, of what we hoped would soon be our land. The birch trunks we had pulled across the entrance back in March were still there. Several new small green saplings were eagerly growing in the middle of the trail. It looked so much more overgrown; I was wondering how we would get the trailer in without some serious pruning.

Eager to explore, I jumped out of the truck. "Come on, let's take a look."

"Wow, look at how much has grown," Dave said as he waded into the trail. The ferns were hip-deep, crowding the open areas between the trees.

"Listen to that," I said.

"What? I don't hear anything."

"Exactly." That was one thing I loved about this place. Even with direct access off the highway, there was little road noise most of the time. We were about 15 minutes' drive from the ferry. Meaning the only noise was a brief rush of traffic every 30 minutes and then very few cars until the next dash for the ferry.

"Shall we take a walk and see where we want to park the trailer?" we were keen to get set up. It seemed sensible to scope out the area on foot first, as we could not remember what the trail was like if it was suitable to drive on, or how far it went. I was reluctant to pull the trailer in and get stuck somewhere without turning around. We were pretty sure we would need to reverse the trailer, so it was not blocking the exit for the truck.

Dave looked at the entrance. “We’ll need to trim down these shrubs.”

He pointed to the recent growth that threatened to overgrow the rough track winding into the property.

I nodded, walking on. The driveway, if you could call it that, veered right at first and then looped gradually left, giving an effective screen from the road very quickly. It headed in an easterly direction, towards the rear of the property. A quick scan of the ground, I could see it was mixed fine gravel and seemed almost like someone had built it as a driveway in the past. Reasonably level and free from ruts and potholes. It would be a perfect surface to drive in with no additional work required. As we rounded the curve, the driveway straightened, and the trees thinned into a beautiful sunny spot filled with ferns.

“How about parking here to start with? It’s far enough, so it shelters us from the road. It’s nice and level, and we’ve got some sun.” I said to Dave.

“Looks perfect. There’s a tree fallen across the trail farther up, so this is probably a good starting point.”

We headed back; I was eager to get the trailer in position. Reversing the trailer was my job, as Dave wasn’t much practiced at it. I didn’t mind, but I would be glad when it was in place. As we stepped out to the gravel, a pickup truck pulled in beside us.

“Do you have permission to be on this land?” a grizzled, bearded man asked. Not overly friendly, but neither rude.

Dave answered, "Yes, we do," and explained the details of our buying it. So, it introduced us to our first neighbour Matthew (Mat) Hauser, who owned the five acres to the right of us. We felt quite reassured that someone was looking out and checking on who was coming and going. He introduced his grandson, daughter, and son-in-law, who were with him. We were welcome to use his driveway to access the back of our property, as he had a much more developed drive. He didn't live there, but rented a place off a side road behind our place and was planning to build a house and move in at some point in the future.

Just as Mat was going, another vehicle stopped, and we met our second set of neighbours within ten minutes of arriving. Brett lived on their 5-acre farm, just to the left of us, with his wife and family, three little girls. Keen to get the trailer parked up, we vowed to catch up and get to know them over the next few days as Brett was rushing to get to the store in Edgewood before it closed.

Chapter Eleven: Camp No 1.

We quickly reversed and then easily unhitched the trailer. After that, levelling up the trailer took minimal effort. We had brought hand tools, spades, and long-handled pruning shears, which helped clear the path. Camp chairs arranged, beer in hand, we cheered our arrival.

Looking around at the wide range of tree species, pines, cedar, fir, birch, hemlock, and larches, heights up to 100 feet. We could see it was a second-growth forest, with huge cedar stumps buried in the uneven ground. Deep potholes merged with the undergrowth from previously ripped out tree stumps. The complete five acres were mostly level, with several old dry stream beds snaking their way between the trees. Everywhere we looked, fresh saplings of every type were shooting up, competing for space. We could imagine the river had run through here in the past, depositing round river rock, sand, and gravel. The river was long gone and now half a kilometre across the roadway over to the left across more grass fields.

Dave got the solar panel set up, battery charging, propane on, and fridge stocked and cooling. Our trailer has fold-out canvas beds, which were luxurious after tent camping and backpacking for years before. We finally set up the trailer, having filled the water tanks en route. With the sun warming us, we sat there in the quiet peace, surrounded by nature. It felt like the most perfect place in the world. All the worries and stress over finance and the legalities of the purchase made it all worthwhile in those moments of blissful peace. But we were too excited to sit still for long, wanting to explore, see more of what we had, and plan what to do next.

We had the workshop delivery to get ready for; we had a lead of a phone number of a guy (Blake) who had a farm towards Edgewood and had a tractor with forks who might lift off the pallet for us. Lots of "mights" and "maybes." It wasn't how we normally liked to operate. I wanted to have firm arrangements in place, taking out the uncertainty, but this was all new, and we didn't have a history of contacts to rely on here. Dave gave Blake a call, but he didn't answer, and we'd been advised not to text him, as he never answers text messages. Now what? I was worried the delivery was going to be here tomorrow. It was a lesson in patience for me not being able to sort a problem out directly and to rely on people we didn't know.

We filled our day with clambering through the undergrowth and ferns. Looking for the white triangular survey pegs that marked the corners of the property. It amazed us that all of them were still intact, considering the damp, humid climate, which we thought would have caused them to rot away. However, from Google Earth and the BC Assessment website, we had a good idea of the overall dimensions; it was a rectangle of land stretching west to east, with the SE corner chunk taken out; it gave access to the well of the neighbouring property.

We wanted to mark the area with tape roughly to be sure when we were wandering off outside the property. The south border was easy, as Mat's driveway ran down the entire length, conveniently marking the line between the two properties.

Brett's driveway meandered along the north boundary, sometimes close to our property line, and sometimes hidden by dense bushes and trees. It was a struggle to find a clear path through.

To the west, the gravel pull-out marked the shorter west property line, and the power lines easement easily marked the east boundary. We now had a good sense of the size. In our wanderings, we had also picked a spot to store the pallet and steel building parts. We would access by using Mat's driveway, as the faint trail on our property petered out after 600 feet, about three quarter's of the way in, dead ending at a grass meadow.

Dave's phone rang as we were wrapping up our surveying for the day. It was Blake; Dave looked at me smugly, as if to say told you so. He has way more trust in people wanting to help than I do. Blake was available tomorrow and would bring his tractor with forks when we called with the approximate delivery time. It all came together again.

While completely absorbed in our plans and buying the land, I received a phone call from my mum via WhatsApp. A sobering reminder of life outside our little bubble. She had tried calling me twice, which was not unusual, as we stayed in touch regularly. It was the perfect way to video chat, send pictures, and stay in close contact. Not being able to get hold of me, she left a message that started with "Don't worry," which means you immediately worry. My gran, 94 and still lived on her own on the family farm, had fallen and broken her arm. She was in the hospital and OK, but the hospital was not allowing any visitors because of COVID. She was in the right place to get patched up, but I could only imagine how lost and scared she was feeling. I sent Mum the video we had taken of the land for her to show gran when she could visit. Gran didn't have WhatsApp on her basic cell phone, so it was impossible to talk to her directly. But before her accident, we had been in touch regularly via the landline to catch up. As she had been in farming her whole life, she was very interested in hearing what was happening with our potential land purchase. We had just booked our flights to the UK for March 2022 to be there for Gran's 95th birthday celebration. COVID had stopped my regular visits, and I was looking forward to seeing all my family, especially my gran. I was the oldest grandchild, and we shared a special close bond. I know my move to Canada had been very upsetting for her, but she was also very proud and had never been negative about it. Her firm determination, tenacity, and ability to be so supportive and caring for everyone in our family were character traits I hoped I shared with her. She prayed the pandemic would settle down enough to travel next year and enjoy her birthday celebration with the whole family.

Chapter Twelve: The Building Arrives

The delivery day, another sunny, beautiful fall day. We had a call from the driver that he was making his way down through the Monashee pass and would be with us by noon. Blake was on his way, but there was just a little doubt about whether his front-end loader could manage the weight of the pallet. It seemed we were never without some uncertainties that all would go according to plan.

The truck driver could navigate his huge rig into the gravel pull-out area. Blake maneuvered his machine efficiently with the pallet of steel building parts. Before we knew it, the pallet was gradually making its way to its new home, for what we hoped would be a brief time before we could start construction. There was a pallet of tightly strapped steel arches, a heavy tub of bolts, and two boxes of tie-down brackets. It looked so small and innocent, and we thought surely that it would be an achievable project to get it built. The instruction booklet was comprehensive and seemed straightforward. We wanted the building up to store the trailer in over the winter. Now we were on the wrong side of summer to be starting such an ambitious project.

Blake was younger than I thought. He was very outgoing and had a good understanding of the area from living there his whole life. He gave off this complete sense of being capable of getting anything done. Little did we know at that point how much we would come to rely on his knowledge, experience, and help.

During the off-load, Dave was chatting about our plans for the building and construction, and Blake had plenty of promising ideas to share. All the people we had met in this little valley were so welcoming, friendly, and the best kind of people you could hope to meet. At that point, we had thought little about who we would meet in the process of buying the land. Only coming out of the pandemic, we had seen such a huge influx of people to our hometown of Canmore and a great deal of resistance to tourists. Outsiders are coming in, buying up land, hiking up the prices, making it hard for locals, etc. I was almost scared to tell people where we were from, but we experienced no negativity as "outsiders." Everyone was the exact opposite, most welcoming and interested and very willing to take us at face value.

We felt a profound sense of achievement that evening and that all our worries had been unfounded so far. Everything had worked out OK; with the building delivered safely. We had met our neighbours and received offers of help with nothing expected in return. Now we could think about planning the next stage. Of course, pending the close of the purchase, which had faded into the background a little while we were there. We had cleared a small patch of grass and ferns to set out our chairs by the temporary location for the trailer. I wondered why, as humans, we feel the need to clear and make space for ourselves. That we feel it is our right to cut down and make tidy the grass and ferns that have grown so enthusiastically. I felt a little guilty disturbing the plant life. Apart from the logging many years previously, this land had had nothing done to it. Nature was fully in charge here.

My whole body felt it was being rejuvenated by the very atmosphere around us. To sit and fully absorb with all senses, to hear the breeze rustle leaves, see the crystal blue sky, feel the gentle sun, smell the soil and earthy smell of mushrooms. The outside world was just that "outside" of our little haven in the trees.

Chapter Thirteen: Camp No. 2

During our exploring and wandering, we began to appreciate the landmarks. How the driveway meandered side to side across the lot. The tree at the heart of the land. The grassy meadows, and several dry gullies from long-gone river braids. We realized that although it had felt as if we had initially selected a good camp spot when we first arrived; it was too close to the road and there was a lot more depth and potential farther inwards of the plot.

The old campsite in the meadow we had noticed on our first view of the land was a much nicer location. More quiet, full of sunshine and the perfect spot centred on the acreage. It's funny how familiarity makes an area seem less intimidating, and the faint roadway was navigable. We decided to be adventurous and move the trailer to the meadow. After all, we couldn't camp forever on the driveway, and it felt much nicer to be parked more centrally in the land.

Before hitching up, we needed to address the 60-foot dead tree leaning at a 45-degree angle across the trail. Probably the trailer would have scraped by underneath, but it didn't seem worth the risk. The tree was standing dead, and we reasoned it would not be a liberty to cut it down to make it safe, even though we did not legally own the land yet.

I had never been involved with using a chainsaw or felling trees. The theory of it seemed straightforward. Dave had collected firewood for many years and was comfortable using his chainsaw. It had a small bar, but enough for most of the work we needed to do. But up close, it was a tall tree; I looked at how far away the top would land from the base. It was only about eight inches round and very obvious in which direction it would fall, given the angle. Dave tried it with the axe to start, thinking a few chops and it would just break off. There was a lot of brush around the base, and it would have been a lot of work to clear a space for the chainsaw. Well, it was a lot tougher than it looked and determined it wanted to stay upright. I threw a rope over to help persuade it to lie down neatly along the driveway, but it still wasn't budging. So, eventually, Dave fired up the saw, and in 40 secs, it was down. Our first improvement. How much fun is this? I grinned, looking at Dave.

"That'll make some nice firewood," he said proudly, wielding the chainsaw. It seemed poignant that a beautiful tree had grown for so long and, for who knows what reason, had died and was gently returning to the earth. Were we to be stewards of this land and take care of it? If so, I was determined that it would be with responsibility in favour of the fauna, leaving everything in a healthier condition than before. We were there to encourage robust growth and a flourishing woodland. I wanted to learn about forest management and how to look after these proud, majestic trees that we were lucky enough to share the space with.

We could not avoid removing some trees to make space for our plans, but I was sure we could do this with consideration and work around the biggest and oldest trees.

After all, they were here first and, with help, may be here long after we are gone.

Moving the trailer into the meadow was pretty straightforward. We were continually grateful for how flat the entire area was; the firm, supporting sand and gravel made the drive exceptionally smooth. We had stopped at a campground on the drive from Alberta to fill up the onboard freshwater tank so we didn't want to bump the heavy load around too much.

Campsite number two was so much better than temporarily being parked in the driveway. We had a much larger level area outside the trailer and a safe spot to dig in a fire pit. We enjoyed the routine of setting up camp. Getting the fire going, preparing a meal, cooking over the open fire, and watching the flames dance. By September, the sun was setting earlier. As we watched the last rays disappear, we could feel the chill as shadows spread across the meadow, even though it would not be dark for several hours.

The Inonoaklin Valley runs north to south, with the high mountain ranges visible to the east and west. We saw the sun rise over the Selkirk range at mid-morning and dip behind the Monashee Mountains by nightfall. We were taking particular notice of where the sun was at various times of the day, to earmark potential sites for our eventual home. The days grew shorter in September, signalling the approach of winter. We hoped winter would come later than in Canmore, though it would arrive eventually. I still hoped we would have time to get the workshop constructed to provide the shelter for the trailer.

Chapter Fourteen: Meeting the Neighbours

As we settled in by the fire, waiting for the fire embers to glow ready to cook, Dave glanced back towards the trailer.

"What's that?" he leaned forward, looking over my shoulder. "Is that a bear?"

"Yeah right!" I wasn't about to fall for that.

"No, it is. Quick, get your phone," he gestured.

I turned to peer into the trees, and, just behind the trailer, I saw a medium-sized black bear ambling through the grass. It was paying no attention to us, happily wandering along, head sniffing at the ground occasionally. Dave walked over, rapidly punching his phone screen, trying to snap a picture before the bear disappeared.

"Dave, scare it off. We don't want it hanging around here." I was concerned it might come back.

"It's fine, he knows we are here, and he's got somewhere to go." He took a picture as the bear disappeared toward the neighbour's place. "He was not interested in us; I don't think he was anything to worry about," Dave reassured.

We had seen signs of deer, rabbits, and smaller game, and now our first bear. A timely reminder for us to keep a clean campsite and not leave any food items outside. It was definitely on my mind as we went to sleep that night, very aware of how thin the canvas surrounding our bed area was between us and any wildlife. It surprised me it didn't bother me more, especially if having to get out in the night for a pee. But there was a far greater view at night to make us forget all about potential wildlife encounters. I can't count how many times I had a stiff neck from looking up at the night sky. Stars go on and on forever, and the dark sky displaying the layers and layers of galaxies and stars, how little we are on this planet, and how much more is out there.

We got up when it got light and went to bed at dark. Regardless of the time, it was so easy to be in tune with the sun naturally. No need for alarms or clocks. It was heaven. Waking up at dawn, dressing up against the early morning chill, welly boots kicking through the dew. Waiting for the first rays to hit the tops of the trees and, bit by bit, spread across the meadow, water droplets sparkling on the blades of grass. We imagined where we might start the garden, where we would sit on a porch to catch the first sun? Trying to name all the different varieties of trees. Those were special moments, alone in the silence and feeling at peace with the world.

Even though we had settled on using the trailer as our accommodation for the first few years, there would still be things we needed to develop to stay there in a trailer. Having to rely on bringing all our water, using the sewer system in the trailer, and relying on a solar battery system for power was quite stressful and hard work. Constantly wondering if we would run out of water, or there wouldn't be enough sun to charge the batteries or the tanks would need emptying; it wasn't that relaxing. Back home, we had an unlimited supply of water, power, and heat, and I wanted that here so we could enjoy our time without worrying.

I also wanted to avoid dragging out development for years and years. Dave was at the wrong end of his working career to start in construction. My intention was that we had all these creature comforts sorted so we could come here for pleasure and not always be building.

Chapter Fifteen: The Well

Our next minor project included a well inspection. We did not know if anyone had ever used it before, if there was any water in it, its quality, or how to extract it. All we could see was a 6-inch diameter galvanized pipe extending 24 inches out of the ground, covered by an upturned white plastic bucket.

We used our climbing rope to drop into the pipe, as it was all we had, listening for any sound of the splash of water. Our idea was to measure the length of rope needed to reach the water to work out the depth. Dave was gently lowering the rope; I stood with my ear to the well, waiting to hear something. I wasn't sure what. With only a 6-inch diameter, it was impossible to see far down, so we were relying entirely on sound.

"Wait! I think I heard something different" I wasn't sure if it was just the rope hitting the side of the pipe or a splash.

I jerked the rope a couple of times, hearing a faint splash as the end of the rope hit the water deep inside the well.

"Yes, definitely sounds like water."

We pulled it up and measured 14 feet.

"All right! We've got water!" we were pleased. The ground seemed so dry, and after the fires, we had been sure there would be no water at all. Now to find out how much water. The problem was using a climbing rope as a measure was not ideal. We had difficulty knowing when the rope had reached the bottom of the well. Our best guess is that we hit the bottom around 25 feet, but we don't know for sure. We would need to get something better to measure it more accurately. At this stage, we were simply happy to know we had water!

The well was at the back of our property, the terrain quite different from the thick forest covering most of the five acres. The few scattered trees provided more light for grass to grow in the sandy gravel soil. We were beginning to work out where our neighbour's property lines met. The power line that the landowner had installed before he subdivided the 5-acre lots ran adjacent to the east boundary of our land. There was an easement 10 meters on either side of the line, and then other property boundaries began. With no fences, it was guesswork to the exact locations. We could see a small wood cabin, with a cable connecting it to the power lines directly opposite the power line to us. To the left of our property is another small green plywood shed with a power line. That belonged to Brett and Elayne, who owned the farm. We guessed their power, and the well were close by. While surveying the area, to understand the power connection, we noticed we had company. A young woman wandered over, with a small child on her hip and another girl with a mop of beautiful curly red hair hiding shyly behind her legs.

"Hi," she greeted us, "you must be our new neighbours. I'm Elayne; Brett told me he'd met you."

We made introductions and learned more about their farm and the trials during the recent fire evacuation, and met their three girls. Seemed like a lovely family. As we were chatting, we heard the deep throb of a quad bike; the noise getting louder.

"That sounds like Kevin and Ann" Elayne looked around. "they have the property just across from you, that's their power shack". She pointed to the small wood cabin we had noticed. As we looked over, the quad appeared with a guy driving and a woman hanging on the back, both dressed in camo gear and ball caps.

"Howdy neighbours!" Kevin shouted over the quad engine. Grinning and waving. "we'd heard someone had bought the land" he switched off the quad.

Instantly likable, they explained where their ten acres were in relation to ours; they had owned it for seven years and were deliberately developing as they had time. Keen hunters and visiting from Kelowna every other weekend, they knew the area well. Elayne, needing to tend to the kids, made her goodbyes, and we promised to drop by to see the farm soon. We couldn't believe our luck to be surrounded by so many warm, friendly, and welcoming people. We were concerned that the locals wouldn't welcome us since we were from Alberta. They would connect our arrival with an increase in land prices and the displacement of the locals. We were wrong - Kevin and Ann invited us over for a beer, and we felt lucky to be surrounded by such welcoming people.

Our first trip was rapidly coming to a close, and neither of us wanted to think about going home and back to reality. We had a final task to complete. To mark out where we would build the workshop. The game trail from the meadow campsite went east to the well, with a dry former watercourse in between. This was easy enough to traverse on foot but too steep for a vehicle to drive over. We had placed the building parts across the gully, thinking it would be good to have it at the back of the property, near the well and power line.

Chapter Sixteen: Staking Out

After being there for a while, we realized it would be difficult to navigate the gully with the truck, and we would have to fill it in if we planned to use it regularly. We had the ideal spot for the workshop right in front of us, this side of the gully. Scrubby shrubs, rough grass, and a complete lack of trees characterized the open meadow of our current campsite. We could construct there without removing any large trees, and the driveway came there already, making a good turnaround spot by the workshop.

Dave held the tape as we measured out the space and tapped in four stakes with orange marker tape. Now that we had the spot, it would enable Blake to start the excavation once we had completed the sale, without us having to be there.

Neither Dave nor I had ever worked with such a blank canvas before and to choose where to position things was challenging . It was so hard! To pick a spot to start from, most times, you move into a home or property where someone else has already cleared it and decided where everything will go. You just have to work with what is already there. Here, we had so much space to work with, we could orient buildings in any direction, and we had no power lines, water pipes, or any services to work around. We were totally in control of where everything would be. That made it more difficult. Every time we walked around, we found a new perfect spot. We needed vision and imagination to see beyond the undergrowth and trees that were there; I couldn't imagine how each spot would look if we cut a tree down or built a building there.

In a flurry of inspiration and encouraged by the workshop stakeout, we appraised the area for potential cabin sites. We wanted to stay as central to the property as possible, keeping maximum privacy from the surrounding acreages. Also, use the driveway that was already roughed in and consider the inventory of trees. When walking east along the drive from the front of the land, just before the meadow opened up on the left, was a trio of white-barked birch trees on the right. Each tree had two or three trunks sprouting up from the base. What had caught Dave's eye was another tall dead pine lodged precariously at the top of one of these birches—more potential firewood. I feared it would damage the birch, known for rotting and trunks shattering, so we had the chainsaw ready. The three birches grouped in a triangle with a decent-sized cedar nearby were beautiful. All carpeted with a gentle sea of green ferns below. It would be a handsome view from the deck to admire looking west towards the setting sun. We ventured in, and the dew on the fronds immediately soaked our knees. We noticed that the land had a slight elevation and felt rocky under our feet. The tree cover was so thick that it was hard to see beyond it, but with some pruning, we could open up the vista. We may even open it up enough to see the sun setting over the Monashee Mountains.

With orange tape in hand, we marked a 14-foot radius. Because of the rocky nature of this spot, there were no trees within our circle. I had in mind that perhaps a yurt would be an option for our dwelling because of its semi-permanent nature and kit form, making it an easier option to erect. It fitted nicely into the space and would be close enough to the workshop but not in the direct line of the site. We examined the spot from all angles; it seemed worth leaving to let the idea settle in. Before we had arrived, we decided to leave the trailer here, as we planned to be back soon, and it would save having to tow the trailer back and forth. Hearts heavy and a new set of memories and experiences to cherish, we headed home to find out what was happening with the close of the purchase.

I was very lucky to have a most valuable resource to call upon, my dad. In fact, without his advice, support, and solid presence, we might never even have gotten to this stage. My childhood on a farm in England taught me many practical skills - building, mending, growing, and more. Even though it would be years later, I came to appreciate this. It may seem strange to say that we are a close family, given that I had lived in Canada for almost 20 years and had seen my family at most for one brief visit a year. Long-distance calls were all we had before, but now we have high-speed internet, cell phones, and social media for easier communication. Thank you, WhatsApp, for bringing us all closer! I had the luxury of consulting with Dad at every step of the project so far. His wisdom was instrumental in helping us with decisions about the workshop and ideas for the concrete foundation yet to come.

Chapter Seventeen: Running Out of Time

Until Sept 8th, we had received no updates regarding the paperwork through the BC courts. But we had already begun planning the workshop's construction.

I reached out to some contractors to talk with them about the concrete foundation for the workshop. After supplying the drawings, the answer was discouraging and alarming in several ways. The contractor was too busy to schedule anything until the spring and the cost for the preparation and completion of the concrete was over $15,000. This was much more money than we had imagined it would cost. We couldn't afford that kind of money and even if we had the money, the timescales were unacceptable as we needed the work done before winter.

By the middle of September, we still had yet to hear from the lawyer, Sarah, or our finance adviser. It was getting alarming, after all our efforts, and we had no control over this part. There was nothing we could say or do that would make any difference, and the window of time to get the workshop built was closing.

Continually on the lookout for items that might be helpful, a garden friend of mine offered us a 1000-litre IBC water storage tank as they didn't need it anymore. "IBC" is short for Intermediate Bulk Container. A large, white plastic container surrounded by an aluminum cage, used for transporting liquids. They had used this IBC in their backyard to collect rainwater off the house roof, to water their garden. All we had to do was remove it from their backyard. I gathered up some of my son's friends as 'volunteers'. We surveyed the spot. The rainwater collector had been in place for a long time behind their house, hidden along a narrow-overgrown pathway. After an enormous struggle, broken branches, and scraped knuckles, the tank was in the back of the truck. Piled high with tools, building materials, tarps, and all manner of items we expected we might need. Never again would the truck be empty on a trip to BC.

The weather had cooled quite a lot since our previous visit; grey clouds shrouded the mountains, the air heavy with moisture. It drenched our shoes and legs every time we stepped out of the trailer. We offloaded and wrapped everything in tarps to keep the wood dry until we needed it. The pallets and lumber we had rescued from various job sites it was amazing what waste materials were available. Contractors were happy to give it away to avoid landfill fees. Despite not owning the land yet, we planned for the future.

I had invited my son Oliver to come with us on this trip. He lived with his dad, and at 19 years old, I didn't get as much time to spend with him as I would like. It was a pleasant opportunity for a road trip. He enjoyed camping, but this level of off-grid camping was not his thing; I wondered what he would think of it. As there was a limited amount we could do on the property, we went exploring. To get to know the area and discovering the nearby swimming holes as options for summer activities next year. While he was politely interested, I could not imagine him helping much unless we had quad bikes or snowmobiles to make it more fun. It was only to be a brief trip, to show Oliver the area, but by chance ended up being even quicker than we expected.

Highway 1 through the Kicking Horse Pass was getting a major upgrade and was subject to some overnight closures. We had been monitoring the alerts because if we timed our trip correctly, we could avoid the diversion, which added an hour and a half to an already long journey. Selection of a departure time seemed simple enough, but with two ferry crossings and a time zone, change was not as easy as it sounds. If the ferry was full or delayed, it would mean we didn't catch the right ferry, and the entire trip could take an extra two hours.

Oliver had been calculating how long it would take to get home, so we could work out what time to get up, to catch the ferries. Google, in her infinite wisdom, told him it would be 8.5 hours to get home, which was significantly longer than the typical 6-7 hours we expected. Then he realized it was directing us via Radium because of the road closure. So, we had a dilemma. If we left tomorrow morning as planned, it would be an extra long trip, or if we left right away this evening, we could make it through before the road closed at midnight. The latter would be a quicker journey home but would create a chaotic hour to pack up everything to leave so suddenly in time to get through before the road closed. What to do? We had to go early tomorrow anyway, so there was no advantage to staying another night. We rushed to finish our meal, put away the beds, clean the fridge, discard the food, get the battery, and make sure everything was secure. Then it was a dash for the first ferry and a race through Nakusp and onward for the second ferry; we made it! Our headlights picked out Revelstoke and up to Rogers Pass. We made good time until rain and sleet made traffic slow. Ahead, brake lights glowed red in the spray and we stopped. Anxiously watching the clock and GPS navigation system with the predicted time of arrival in Golden, the minutes stretched out. Would we make it in time? Maybe they will delay closing the road… we'll make it for sure. It was dark, raining, and the worst conditions for driving at night. At ten minutes past midnight, we rolled into Golden to see the orange lights flashing and the road closed sign. All our efforts and rushing had been in vain; we missed it by ten minutes. They left us with no other option but to take the alternative route via Radium, a long winding drive, and took us ten hours to get home. It was the early hours of the morning by the time we made it back to Canmore. We will pay more attention to road closures next time. The distance from Canmore and the time taken to get there and back was certainly adding more challenge to this project than we had considered. I couldn't help wondering at this point if it was going to be manageable.

Chapter Eighteen: The Closing Date

Then it suddenly felt like all the cogs finally meshed, which happened quickly at the end of September. The lawyer casually emailed to say the courts had approved the resealing and set a date of Oct 8 for the close date. Despite the delays, the last transaction went off without a hitch. The credit union got the funds transferred, and the land was now officially ours. So many months of sleepless nights wondering if it would all come together and if our dream would become a reality. I eagerly anticipated going back. Looking forward to wandering through the trees, surrounded by our little haven filled with ferns. We could finally start making actual plans without worry of it never being a reality. It was amazing to shed the feelings of anxiety, the ifs, and maybes, and dare to look to the future.

The future. What would that be? Now that we had the property, what did we really want to do with it? Would this become a full-time home? Would we visit for summer trips? So far, Dave had been supportive, but had not been the initiator. I have always been forward-thinking and a planner, looking to the future. I have been lucky enough to always know what I want, formulate plans to take action, and achieve those goals. Dave was more reactionary, living in the moment and planning day by day, without a long-term plan. From the start of our search, Dave and I were coming to this new venture from quite different perspectives. I had some concerns about what effect our differences may have and if our unspoken expectations were not in alignment. Dave knew it was a lifelong dream of mine to have a piece of land and was willing to help me achieve this. But I wondered how much he wanted all this stress and hassle of making it a reality. Dave is twenty years my senior, very fit, active and you would never know this from looking at him. I wondered how fair I was being, expecting him to take on such a project when he should look forward to a more leisurely lifestyle. He liked the idea of the investment and owning land; I liked the idea of building a cabin and living in the woods, and was prepared to learn whatever I needed to and do the work ourselves. I was against paying someone else while I was working to pay them. Dave, on the other hand, did not have the building skills and felt more inclined to earn money to pay someone for the hard labour required. How were we to compromise on these opposites?

At this point in the project, we just wanted to own the land, which had already seemed enough of a hurdle. But I was already thinking ahead about what would come next.

We filled our time at home in Canmore with planning, researching, and learning all that we could. Working out what to do next. While we had the luxury of the trailer to stay in, we did not want to have to haul the trailer off-site to empty the grey and black water tanks. The nearest sani-dump was the other side of the ferry crossing. We needed an outhouse. We had a large amount of waste lumber, including plywood, 6x6 posts, and many 2x4s, only needing to buy a few additional items. This was our first experiment at building anything. I watched a few YouTube videos on building an outhouse and drew some sketches with measurements based on the wood we had.

I've mentioned "watching a few YouTube videos" as a resource, but that is a colossal understatement. There are a few channels I subscribe to that have been invaluable to us. Not just for the tips and knowhow, but also for the inspiration and motivation. One of my most personal favourites is "Girl in the Woods" created by Brooke Whipple and also her husband Dave Whipple's channel "Bush Radical". I absolutely love both of them, their story, their skills and everything they share. Our outhouse was inspired by Dave Whipple's video of outhouse building. What these guys have achieved is amazing. They have been hugely influential. There are too many videos on their channels to mention specific ones here, all of them are fantastic.

Chapter Nineteen: The Outhouse

The truck fully loaded up with construction materials, and we were on the road again. We timed our trip to coincide with highway one being open, as it was the thanksgiving weekend. Cautiously watching the weather forecast, we might be lucky enough to get our project completed without getting too wet.

As we pulled in, it felt different. The land was finally ours. It was surreal that after all the obstacles and delays that we had experienced; I was sure it would never come true. I found it difficult to remember a time when I had wanted something so badly. The only thing I can come close to comparing it to was emigrating to Canada 20 years previously. That had taken five years of planning to organize, so this was a much shorter timescale, yet had felt equally stressful.

Everything looked as we had left it, even given the rushed exit of our last trip. The area is prone to opportunist thieves, and there was always a worry that the materials and tools accumulating might not be there when we got back each time. So far, we have been lucky. We had nowhere secure to store anything. We protected the materials and tools from the weather by stuffing it under the trailer or wrapping it in a tarp.

It was beginning to look like a junkyard, with building materials, pallets, water tanks, and tools.

The ferns had turned brown and trees were looking autumnal into October. Yet the BC climate felt much milder than the sharp frosts already frequent at home in Alberta. It was getting chilly staying in the trailer with the canvas pull-out beds at night, but the days were still relatively warm. With lots of trees for shelter, the wind passed over our little haven. By Saturday morning, I was up early to look around for a suitable spot for the outhouse. Once again, the number of possibilities was overwhelming. We could pick anywhere, but would we regret it later on? What if it turned out to be too close to something else or not near enough?

Dave came to the rescue with his logic and analytical mind. "How about over there?" he pointed to a spot at the edge of the trees across the driveway from the potential yurt site. "It's equal distance from the yurt, the workshop, and out of the way of anything else."

It seemed good, and I needed someone else to confirm a suitable spot. Shovels, gloves, and pickaxe in hand, we were eager to begin. Well, perhaps eager to get it finished was a more accurate description. We had no notion of the time required to dig a 3 x 3 feet hole six feet deep, the level of difficulty involved, or its feasibility in the soil.

I volunteered first shift. It was pretty hard getting the shovel to bite in through the tough shrub roots, and slow going. If this is indicative, I thought to myself, this is going to take a long time. The first six inches felt like I was using an egg cup to scrape away at the surface. Then, as the blade cut through the top layer of fibrous roots, I began to make more progress. The shovel cut through the sandy soil, pulling up complete shovelfuls every time. Clang, then a jarring halt as it hit a large rock. It took some maneuvering to get the shovel in the correct position but wasn't too difficult to remove. There were a lot of very round river rocks, and once you could get the blade's edge down the side of the rocks, they popped out easily. Extremely dense and heavy, it was easier to lift them out by hand as the hole got deeper.

Dave took his turn, and we were making substantial progress. It quite encouraged us by the pile of dirt growing and the three feet hole we had excavated. There is a strange satisfaction in digging a hole manually; you can get into a routine, of chipping away with the shovel to loosen the dirt, then levering each shovelful up and out, then chipping away again and lifting it out. As the hole gets deeper, it's harder to get much dirt with each lift, but slowly and surely, every bit taken out of the hole is a step closer to the depth we wanted. As we dug through a layer of sand, the sides of the hole began to collapse, and each shovelful out resulted in more sand falling in.

"This is not getting us anywhere; the hole is shallower than it was ten minutes ago," I said, getting frustrated. "We need to shore up the sides."

But how? I had an idea. We could use some of the stripped-down pallets to build a box that would line the hole, holding back the side walls. Like extras from the Great Escape, we built our box to hold up our vertical tunnel and rammed it down into the hole. Once again, chipping away and removing dirt from the centre of the hole. It worked! No more side collapse, and we got closer and closer. As the hole deepened, we could push the box down farther to hold the sides back. Finally, we were at the depth we wanted. It was pretty hard to get out of the hole. "That's the last time we will ever want to be down in this hole," I stated, as Dave helped pull me out.

The next stage involved levelling two 6-inch by 6-inch beams about six feet in length parallel to each other as a foundation for the walls. We had pre-cut the side walls for the outhouse from sheets of plywood, rescued from building sites back in Canmore. Framed with 2-inch by 4-inch lumber, it encouraged us by how quickly it took shape. I found a plan online that we were loosely following with some modifications.

With no power, we had to make do with cordless tools, with chargeable batteries that we hoped would last until the project was done. Finally, the circular saw gave up, and we resorted to using the chainsaw for a few last cuts. Once we secured the side walls and roof, we built a boxed-in seating area, cut out the hole, and attached a regular toilet seat for comfort and easier cleaning.

A great tip we learned online was to use off-cuts from the roofing material as a splash guard. To ensure all liquids drained down into the hole instead of soaking into the wood and causing typical outhouse smells. This was the first structure we had ever built, and there were few issues; in a little over two days, our outhouse was complete. Clear plastic sheets on the roof let in light. We made the door from recycled pallet boards with a uniquely shaped branch handle.

We looked over to admire our handiwork, feeling a proud sense of achievement. With effort and hard work, we had built it entirely from upcycled wood. Our first structure and we finally had a dry place to store tools.

Before this, we had stuffed everything under the trailer, hoping it would not rain too hard and the tarps would keep the chainsaw and hand tools safe. Now, what luxury! We could place items inside a small, cluttered building and close the door, and they would be safe from the elements. It was a declaration and stamp on the land, claiming it—our first step towards independence and being able to have everything we needed right there to survive.

Chapter Twenty: Workshop Prep Work

The season was catching up with us, and it was getting colder. Keeping warm in the trailer required extra layers and not drinking in the evening to save having to step out into the frosty night for a pee. But at least we had a beautiful outhouse when nature called, even if it was a chilly dash across the meadow.

We met with Blake just before the end of our trip to discuss the excavation for the workshop foundation. He would make a start on it while we were away and had two guys who would build the formwork for the concrete.

We needed to move the trailer out of the construction zone and found a level clearing, about halfway down the drive between the workshop site and the road. It felt that every time we got settled in a camp spot; the trailer was uprooted again, and dragged off between a new area of bushes, ferns, and saplings. The latest spot was far from idyllic but necessary, and we consoled ourselves with the knowledge it would not be for long. Not knowing how much frost-free time we would have left, we needed to winterize the trailer to prepare for colder weather ahead. As it was our first year as trailer owners, we were unsure how to do this. In theory, it seemed straightforward. Buy a jug of trailer antifreeze, pump it through all the pipes until the pink stuff ran out the faucets, and we'd be done. But with only the trailer battery power source and not knowing how to disconnect the water pipes we were seriously ill equip. We opted for a quick solution that we knew was not ideal, but we'd deal with that problem next year when we weren't in the middle of the foundation crisis. After draining the fresh water tank, we poured the winterizing fluid into the fresh water tank; powered by the battery, we used the trailer water pump and opened all the faucets until the pink stuff was running. Winterization done! Even though we would have to flush the fresh water tank next year thoroughly before using it.

We had noticed a leak inside the trailer as water spots dripping on the dining table on and off, which was becoming more noticeable in the rainier BC climate. Sealing the dried-out caulking and covering the trailer in a tarp was necessary to avoid winter damage. Now the interior of the trailer would be dry, whatever rain or snow was in the forecast.

Back home and back to the workshop, concrete foundation problem-solving. We sourced another contractor who offered a more reasonable quote, but only for pouring and finishing the concrete. As we now had Blake working on the excavation and groundwork prep, it felt like the team was coming together. My optimistic plan was to have the groundwork and formwork, and rebar in place for the concrete pour on November 15th. Which gave us almost a month, and with Blake and his two guys, it seemed very doable.

We would arrive a few days before to make sure everything was in place and ready for the concrete pour.

We received a comprehensive package of engineered drawings, plans, and instructions with the purchase of the workshop. Originally, we had been hoping to pass these on to the contractor who would build the foundation and erecting the building. However, now that we were taking a more hands-on approach to the project, I had taken over as project manager and was very grateful for the level of detail. My dad and I spent many an hour on WhatsApp, again relying heavily on my dad's experience and knowledge in building farm buildings and construction,; me picking his brains on what we would need and how to get ready.

I could now understand why the contractor's quote was high. There was excavation, and a concrete pad embedded with a complex pattern of metal reinforcement. Plus two channels running parallel down each side of the concrete pad to hold the steel walls of the building.

I had been studying the workshop build instructions and drawings calculating the amount of rebar required. Ordering rebar from Vernon, with all pieces bent to the correct angles and delivered to the site, proved to be impossible. As it was such a small project, no company was interested in even quoting for the work. Our only option was to buy the lengths of rebar from our local builders' yard and get Blake's guys to fit it in place as part of the formwork building.

Our project was one of many things Blake was working on, and he had delegated the work to his two guys. We had exchanged a few texts regarding progress and were shocked when they said they had done all they could and were heading to Costa Rica for the winter. They hadn't delivered the rebar yet. Oh, and by the way, could we e-transfer their wages?

We were going to be there the following week and wondering how we would be ready for concrete. Anxiously watching the weather, amazingly, it was looking mild with no frosts or snow in the forecast. We might just be lucky.

We were certainly learning a lot. Out of our comfort zone again, but I was determined to get this concrete done; I wanted a secure place to keep our trailer in.

Chapter Twenty-One: Unpleasant Surprise

I couldn't believe another month had slipped away since we were here last. But the low sun had relentlessly stolen daylight hours, and the cold made everything much more challenging. It was always so exciting to pack up a new load of supplies, our imagination making simple work of what we would build with it. Funny how optimism refuses to acknowledge our shortcomings and how challenging and physical the work might be. This trip we brought with us new tools. Wood for the pumphouse. A rented rebar bender (a strange yellow long-handled awkward device I could not for the life of me work out how it was supposed to work). Insulated tarps to cover the concrete once poured (in case of frost). The rental shop in Canmore had suggested a propane heater for the tarps, but it was too overwhelming to contemplate setting all that up; we would take our chances.

The trailer was still there, not spirited away by opportunistic thieves, safely dry under the massive tarp. It was always a relief to find everything precisely as we had left it.

Very concerning for us, the excavations and foundation prep work were as we had left them. There was a shallow hole in the ground, with two deeper trenches running the length of each side. Some rough-cut lumber scattered in the grass, and a green bin bristling with sharpened stakes all ready for some undetermined purpose.

Since our last visit, they had completed three hours of work. It was hard to prevent panic from overwhelming us and we surveyed the site. Everything would all be OK; Blake would be here tomorrow, and we would still have enough time to prepare. After all, all we had to do was get the crushed rock in place, compact it, build the wooden formwork, level, and square it. Then get the rebar cut, bent, and secured in place. Then build the keyway formwork (the two channels running lengthways down each side that the steel arches of the building would rest in.)

"Don't worry, we can do it" my mind was in action mode. We would do it because we had no choice. We had concrete ordered, and a crew scheduled to be here in four days. This may not have seemed like too big of a deal for an experienced and knowledgeable cribbing crew. I was uncomfortable having to depend heavily on Blake for help. I was uneasy having to be so reliant upon someone else being able to commit and help us out.

We dumped out the tarps and rebar bender and looked on helplessly, unsure what to do first. It was already getting dark on day one. Finally, we retreated to the trailer, tried to get warm, and keep our spirits up and minds focused on the task ahead. My mind ran through all the steps, rehearsing what we needed to get done.

Chapter Twenty-Two: The Foundation

The next morning, it was just about getting light by 8 am; we were at the job site, as they delivered the rebar. Step one, good start; we now had some tangible tasks to work on. If we could only understand how this rebar bender works. We didn't have any spare rebar for mistakes. I had already prepared a detailed plan for our needed lengths and angles. The long lengths of rebar were heavy and dangled awkwardly as we heaved them into place. It took a bit of manhandling, and pretty soon we were churning out squares of bent rebar like giant misshapen horseshoes. They clanged into a growing pile as we mentally counted off the number we needed. I wouldn't say they looked very professional at all, but it was quite satisfying to see the pile grow and know it was one less task.

By the time Blake was reversing his truckload of crushed rock to the site, we had most of the rebar cut and shaped. They soon distributed the hardcore with his Case loader and spread it within the excavated hole. Blake also provided a heavy-duty compactor to provide an adequate base for the concrete. It was too large for this particular task, but we could not be choosy at this point. It got the job done once they fired the big diesel engine into life. With heavy black fumes spewing, it produced enough vibration to pack the crushed rock as hard as concrete. I was happy Rick was holding onto the thing as he wrestled with it across the pad.

"Time to call it a day. We'll be back tomorrow with more wood for the formwork," Blake said.

It surprised me to realize the light was already fading. We trudged back to our trailer, too tired to prepare a meal. It didn't seem worth sitting around trying to stay warm, so we went to bed and, hopefully, to sleep and forget about workshop foundations for a little while.

We were again lucky to see another dry morning, the ground hard with frost but not enough to freeze our water container in the trailer yet. BC had issued a severe weather warning of wet and windy conditions as an atmospheric river was dumping rain from the west coast and reaching as far as us. All around us, roads were closed because of washouts and mudslides, yet the sun was out right here, and the arduous work was enough to have us shedding our jackets by 10 am.

We soldiered on, and the site was finally beginning to take shape. Blake had provided some lumber from his sawmill. Massive thick lengths, heavy and sturdy enough to run the full 24-foot length of the workshop base. He used his laser level and impact driver to secure the pieces of shoring together. We methodically staked and bolstered up the shoring, ready for the weight of the concrete. By the end of the day, we had the rectangular formwork in place. Leaving us with two days to get the concrete reinforcement in place and figure out how to build the keyway formwork. That was a puzzle I had asked as many people as I could, but no one had come up with a workable suggestion that I thought we could build with what we had. The keyway was integral to ensuring the steel arches would be structurally sound and in the right position.

One thing I was coming to expect is that there is no point in wasting time trying to anticipate and worry about every detail beforehand. We just had to jump in and get started. There almost always was a minor thing I had overlooked that caused the biggest delays and problems in our work. When working on things we had never done before or knew nothing about, no amount of preparatory work or research could make us sure of the outcome.

The keyway and all the work I had put in to find a solution to this problem, and we were down to the line and still did not know how to do it. No one we asked had any idea either. We would just have to make something.

Chapter Twenty-Three: Rain

Blake was keen to get back to his work, and there was little else he could help with until we figured out the keyway problem. Dave and I were on our own, the responsibility of the project weighing heavily. At least we could get the rebar in place while thinking about it. The drizzle began to fall as we started the laborious task of installing the rebar that would reinforce the concrete.

Bent over in a growing puddle of water as the rain got heavier and heavier, we had no choice but to continue. By noon, we had half of one side finished. Water running off our pants drenched our socks inside our boots as the heavy rain soaked us through. It was not icy rain, just very persistent. I forced my wrinkled fingers inside sopping leather gloves to keep twisting wires for the rebar. We concentrated on the rebar and developed better methods of measuring, cutting, bending, and fastening. Finally, the pile of rebar squares disappeared into the structure, and in the failing light of day three, it was complete.

We splashed back to the trailer in the dark, stripped off dripping clothes, and shivered into sleeping bags with a hot water bottle. I poured out my boots, hoping they might dry a little overnight. It surprised me when Dave said its only 6 pm; it felt like midnight.

I could not imagine how Dave was feeling; he had not wanted to be involved in the construction and had wanted to get contractors to help. Now here we were, inexperienced, uncomfortable, and under a deadline of my making, in which he had no alternative but to keep going and help. I was full of admiration at his fortitude and stoicism; if our positions had been reversed, I would have been giving him a much harder time.

Stiff and aching, it took some courage to shrug back into wet jackets, boots, and gloves the next morning. It was still raining. I had been working on an idea for the keyway, but we needed more lumber. Luckily, it was one of the two days a week the builder's merchant was open. We precariously balanced long lengths of lumber out the back of the truck for the brief journey back. Fortunately, we could get lumber locally without that; I'm not sure what we would have done. By now we were operating on autopilot, not feeling the rain or how uncomfortable it was, just focused on completing the formwork. Once we had puzzled out how to construct the first channel and attach it to the outside forms, with supports underneath, the second keyway went more quickly. In the dim, damp afternoon, I straightened up, my back creaking, and realized it was done. We were ready for concrete. Such relief that our part was done. The concrete finishers would be in charge tomorrow and we could watch from the sidelines. Completely exhausted, we stood, rain dripping off our noses, and looked at each other, too tired to move.

I smiled. "We did it Dave. Would you ever have imagined you'd be doing this when you met me?" It wasn't something I would have imagined doing either. I knew that at some point, we would look back with wonder at how we managed it. But little did we know this was just the start and there would be much more blood, sweat, and tears before we could relax.

Chapter Twenty-Four: Concrete Pour

The day dawned brighter, dry and a few degrees above freezing; the sullen grey sky seemed wrung out and too tired to rain anymore. Jaz texted to confirm he was en route. We had confirmed with the concrete company in Nakusp that the truck had left the plant and was on its way to the ferry.

Jaz pulled up and began unloading a wheelbarrow and tools.

"Good morning, nice to finally meet you; thank goodness the weather is cooperating so far," I introduce myself to Jaz, "are the other guys coming in another vehicle?"

"Oh no, it's just me. This isn't that big a job; I'll be able to get this done on my own," he said.

My body groaned, realizing that we would be pitching in if we wanted a good finish on the concrete. There was no way one guy could wheelbarrow, tamp, and place an entire load of concrete on his own. He didn't even have a concrete vibrator to de-air the concrete. There wasn't much time to consider the options. Dave was at the driveway entrance guiding the concrete mixer truck, and I heard the faint beep of the reversing signal. Slowly, the huge concrete truck maneuvered the narrow driveway.

The truck driver got set up. Jaz dragged his single wheelbarrow beneath the chute, and we were underway. Concrete in a wheelbarrow is extremely heavy, and as Jaz heaved each barrow full to the far end of the pad, we were ready with rakes and shovels to push it into place. It took about two hours to pour the full load of concrete into place. Then the truck had a three-hour turnaround time to return to Nakusp for the second load.

Even though the watery sun was peaking through the clouds in our little sheltered spot, we were unaware the rest of BC was fighting gales and torrential rain. Mudslides had closed Highway one and many of the major routes from Vancouver and traffic was being diverted to Highway 6 and across the ferries. We had not noticed the increased noise and volume of cars streaming by. Luckily, concrete delivery gets priority on the ferry, so the truck could skip the two-hour wait for the ferry. We only realized the traffic chaos when the truck arrived back, with the second load reporting on the long wait lines.

Floodwater swamped entire regions of the Fraser Valley. They issued evacuation orders for many communities, including Merritt, Princeton, and Abbotsford. As of November 17th, the province declared a state of emergency, stating that the storm was the worst weather to hit the area “in a century”.

As Jaz finished the surface, fat spots of rain pattered holes in the fresh surface, and we quickly pulled over the tarps to minimize the damage. By then, we were not too worried about the finish on the surface and relieved it was all done. What a relief to put this stage behind us and look over the white tarps completely cocooning our lovely fresh concrete floor.

The sun was innocently spreading her warmth the following day. Showing no remorse for the misery she had put us through with her absence over the previous few days. We pulled back the tarps with intrepidation, wary of standing on the freshly poured concrete.

Dave tapped his boot lightly against the surface. "Do you think it's hard enough to stand on?"

"I should think it's OK" I stepped onto it. It was solid. I scraped my boot just to test how hard it was. I couldn't see even the faintest mark from my boot.

"It's good; I guess we should loosen up the keyway formwork before it gets too hard to move," I said.

We had not been able to oil the wood used for the keyway and it was going to be challenging to get it out as concrete surrounded it on three sides. Even after only 24 hours, it was another lengthy, frustrating process trying to lever out the wood. In the beginning, we were carefully trying to tap the wood to break it free from the concrete. But after a couple of inaccurate blows to the concrete, where the hammer just bounced right off, we became less cautious. We eventually removed the wood from the channels and discovered two perfectly parallel channels running down each side of the pad.

"That looks quite professional" impressed by our work, not bad for two newbie cribbers. We had done a respectable job; we had every right to be proud. It had been arduous work and not what we had intended to spend the week doing. But we had done it and worked hard for it—saving ourselves several thousand dollars in the process. We left the insulated tarps in place to ensure the curing concrete stayed above freezing to give it a chance to gain maximum strength.

We headed back to Canmore and back to a completely different world. Where our challenges comprising what to watch on TV, who was going to the grocery store, or what to eat for dinner. Our bodies took longer to recover, muscles and hands aching from doing unfamiliar manual labour. There was great satisfaction in having faced up to a significant task, both physically and mentally. Not only overcoming the challenge, but having a solid structure in place to show for all our efforts. Made even more rewarding because we were not construction workers or tradesmen with any experience at all. Not bad for a middle-aged woman who writes safety manuals and a 70-year-old guy who does accounting.

Chapter Twenty-Five: That's a Wrap for the Year

The following week, Oliver, my son, and I made the almost 1200 km round trip to pick up the tarps, to return to the rental place. By then, there was already an inch of snow on them, but the concrete was a week old and had to fend for itself. We loosened up the rest of the formwork, slipping around in the slushy snow. That was to be our last visit of the year. The trailer packed up, locked up and tarped up and left to take its chance against the winter snow. We had hoped to get the workshop up and complete to store the trailer in, but needed more time. Would everything survive the winter intact? We did not know and could only hope for the best.

We had taken an enormous gamble in pushing to get the foundation down before the winter, and against all odds, our naivety had paid off. Usually building projects shut down in November. Because of unpredictable weather and potentially heavy snowfalls, yet we squeezed in under the wire. Even though we had not achieved our goal of fully constructing the workshop, we now had the base ready for construction next year. There would be less pressure, as we would have the entire summer to get it built before the snow came again.

Over the winter, we watched the snow pile up from the trail cam images, faithfully recording even at the lowest temperatures. We expected the batteries to die at some point, but they kept going strong. We had the camera pointed at the tarp-covered workshop kit, reasoning that this was our most expensive item there and better for security. At some points, the snow was a foot deep on top of the tarp, and then it would melt away as temps increased, then another dump would pile up again. The occasional deer walking through triggered an interesting picture. But it was mainly white and peaceful.

Then, as the daylight hours got longer, patches of the ground grew larger as the snow retreated, and it was time to get excited about our first trip back. We were eager to check out the trailer. Before winter, our friends had advised us to use Bounce dryer sheets in the trailer to deter mice and other vermin. Which we hadn't even thought about until that point. We cleared out all the food, soap, and other items that might attract animals. But as we did not point the trail cam at the trailer in its temporary location, we did not know if the trailer was even still there.

The four long, cold, dark months of winter gave us lots of time to discuss what we would like for the following year. Given the distance and time to get there and back, we could not realistically visit for just a weekend at a time. It needed a minimum of four days away, and we took almost two of these days up with travel. I wanted to spend at least ten days at a time there through the summer. Rather than rushing to get there, rushing to get projects done while we were there, and rushing to get home. I could do most of my work remotely so that I could keep up with my work from there. I wanted Dave to be there with me, but as he needed to visit worksites to complete his work, it was difficult for him to get away. He did not want to tell his clients he would be away so much and was reluctant to commit to my plans. This, I translated as a lack of commitment to our project. What was the point of owning this beautiful piece of land if we didn't have enough time to spend there to enjoy it?

I wanted to think about moving there full-time once we had built somewhere to live. Canmore had lost its appeal to me. It was far busier than it used to be, longer colder winters, and the land had so much more opportunity for things to do. Gardens, trees to look after, trails to build, a chance to live more simply and be more self-sufficient. Dave loves Canmore, the lifestyle, the ski hills, golfing and likes to have holidays in BC but not live there and not have to put in work to create a liveable space. We never spoke about this so candidly, as I think we both felt we were not entirely sure what we wanted from this new adventure. There were so many unknowns. So, we kept our thoughts to ourselves and just hoped that by the time we could make changes, it would be more clear what we wanted.

I felt Dave feared the unknown and thought it was too big of a change to move there. But I hoped the more time we spent there, the more he would come to love it and realize it was a lifestyle he could embrace and enjoy. I knew for sure that even to consider such a move, we would need comfortable living quarters with running water, power, and heat. Even I was not prepared to live full time in the trailer. The past few weeks had shown us how uncomfortable that was.

Also, another factor was Dave's age; I wanted us to have everything finished so that we could go there to relax and enjoy some leisure time. Well, more leisurely pursuits like gardening, an outdoor fireplace, or more fun projects that didn't matter if they took a while to finish. Not be constantly working on construction that needed to be done before we had somewhere to sleep. We would need more time and more money to build a cabin realistically instead of spending the little we could save as we earn it. It could take years if we did it that way.

We had to come up with a better plan for 2022, but we just needed to figure out what it would be. Or how we would do it.

On reflection, looking back on our first year of owning the land, it was hard to remember what we did with our time beforehand. We had not realized how much it would change everything. What had we achieved in this first year? We built the outhouse, got the foundation completed for the workshop, cleared some trees, and set up our trailer. These few accomplishments fell short of what I had hoped: to have at least built the workshop to protect the trailer over the winter. The delays with the purchase had cost us too much time if it had even been realistic as a goal. I have a habit of being over-ambitious in my expectations and focusing on what we didn't get done rather than what we have achieved. After all, we only spent 19 nights staying on the land in 2021. Given our lack of experience, skills, and knowledge of the area and the distance from our home, we were happy with what we had learned and achieved. I finally had achieved my dream of owning a plot of land with trees and a blank canvas to create a beautiful place to enjoy. I couldn't wait to get started the next year! Dave said nothing and rolled his eyes. He already knew me well enough to say nothing about my lofty goals and ideas.

We now had several months of planning time. I didn't want to waste this time, having realized how short a season we had; at least next year we would have from April until November far more time than this year. There was so much to think about. What would we do about power, go solar or use the power line and hook up to the grid? How would we get water out of the well? What was our plan for more permanent living? Were we content with the trailer long-term? It had been so cold in there I wanted to visit any time of year and have somewhere warm to stay. How would we afford everything? Save and pay for things as we progress or borrow more money? My mind was full. I just wanted to move forward and get some decision made so it would stop. Dave preached caution. After all, it was months until we would be there again; we didn't need to make hasty decisions or commit to anything at the moment.

Our different approach caused friction. It felt to me like he wasn't interested in the project at all; he never brought up the topic in conversation, and it was me who was doing all the research and collecting information. If we talked about it, I had already thought of or discarded his suggestions because I was working on it every spare minute I had.

"What's the point in me saying anything if you are just going to say that idea won't work?" he said again, options for the well.

"If you spent some time learning and finding out about pumps, you'd know as much as me."

"Oh, you are wonderful, you know everything!" sarcasm dripped off his every word.

"It's not that at all. I'm just pointing out I knew nothing about well pumps before either, but I've spent time learning it. If you took the initiative to learn, you would know these things too" I wanted him to be as interested and enthusiastic as me. But that was the problem he wasn't. I kept having to remind myself of that fact and remember that he was helping me to realize my dream. He didn't want to be doing construction work, working out how to get a septic field built.

He wanted to be planning ski trips, hikes, and golf days. My idea of productivity and enjoyment was building this dream; his priority was on keeping fit and healthy and enjoying leisure time. So how were we going to meet in the middle? Perhaps this was a mistake, and we should sell the place. It was causing too much trouble between us. But every time I thought about being there, the trees, the peace and quiet, slogging around in my wellies (rubber boots) in the early morning dew, and watching the sun touch the treetops. I knew I'd do what needed to be done to make it work.

We were not yet familiar with the seasons and at what time of year it would be possible to access the land, at what point the snow would be gone. We only had our first year experience to go by. There had been very little snow left by March earlier this year and snow had not arrived until December. We planned to return to the land in April of the New Year, as our trip to the UK would take up most of March. My gran, although recovering well from her broken shoulder, was still in hospital. She was desperate to come home, as the pandemic meant she was getting very limited visitors. I could call her regularly, but I was very much looking forward to seeing her in March for her birthday and being able to visit her back at her home.

PART TWO

Chapter Twenty-Six: New Year

Having a trail cam was our only connection to the land over the winter. If any movement triggered a picture, we would get a download daily. If there was no activity, I could request the camera to take a photo at the next download. When the camera took a picture, we got a glimpse of the conditions and temperature at that moment. We saw deer wandering by and the farm cat from next door. Sometimes the snow weighed heavily on the branches, bowing them down to the ground, and other times the snow depth seemed to retreat. All in all, it remained static, a frozen winter wonderland.

As the days got a little brighter and longer, snow disappeared from the trees, and small patches of brown earth appeared. The long, dark winter was finally over. We were not planning to visit again until the middle of April 2022. We had an important family trip to the UK planned for March. My grans 95th birthday. It was an event worth the delay in getting back to the land. She was, unfortunately, still not home from the hospital. They moved my gran from one hospital to another, then to a rehabilitation unit. She had a brief stay at home, but eventually, they had to take her back to the hospital. Pandemic lock down meant she was getting no visitors. It was heartbreaking. Her special birthday, that should have been a big party with family and friends to celebrate, ended up with only a visit from me and Oliver. Only because we came all the way from Canada to see her were, we permitted to enter. I was very grateful we got the chance to visit with her for a few hours. Without that, she would have spent her 95th birthday alone in the hospital. It was so very sad. When the pandemic outbreak was over, I visited her as many times as I could during our stay in England. All too soon, we were flying home to start the next stage of land development.

I couldn't believe that almost five months had passed since we were last there. The logistics of travelling this far required us to arrange longer trips. We could not visit just for weekends. It took six hours to reach our destination and usually took eight hours to return home.

Easter worked well with the extra couple of holidays and we could expect reasonable weather. Truck loaded with supplies, wheelbarrow, water, cordless power tools, and more recycled wood from job sites, we set off with enthusiasm in the early dawn. With clear skies, the bright sun painted the mountains pink, it was a spectacular drive every time. By timing our stops, we could hit the ferry departure times just right and get to the land by late morning.

Chapter Twenty-Seven: Easter Gardens & Ostriches

I breathed a sigh of relief. Our trailer was still there, tarp intact. All was safe and sound, dry, and rodent free. Most of the snow had gone, and the ground was quite dry.

We didn't have many goals for the first trip of the year, except to tidy the concrete workshop foundation and move the trailer onto the concrete. We planned to keep it there until we started constructing the workshop.

I had considered starting a garden, largely as an experiment. We would not be there enough to water it during the dry summer months. It would have to take its chances. From our excavation of the workshop foundations, we knew the soil was poor. We would have to build soil for any decent garden to grow.

Facebook has its pros and cons. I found it a very useful tool for keeping in touch with friends and family wherever they may be in the world. Facebook became an invaluable tool for sourcing materials, information, and ideas. Joining the local community Facebook page when we were buying the land helped us learn about the area and connect with what was happening in the community. A few days before we headed out, I noticed a post from the local ostrich farm selling ostrich manure for the garden. As we arrived, I called them, and we headed over once we'd unloaded the truck to pick up a load. The owner directed us into the field, with about 50 to 100 ostriches strutting around. He jumped in his bobcat and we followed him over to the manure pile. Waiting while he loaded another truck in front of us. His wife cautioned us to stay in the truck and keep moving. If we stopped, the ostriches would think we had food and come over to investigate. They would peck at anything on our vehicle, pulling off the trim and windshield wipers. We idled around, trying not to notice the gathering troop of ostriches following our every move. When this close up, they are a lot bigger and quite intimidating, their beady eyes and expressionless faces staring intently into the truck.

It was at that point I became aware the bed cover was still closed and needed to be opened before we could load up. Unfortunately, it is a manual process that requires stopping and getting out of the truck and folding back the cover. Now we were in the ostrich sights, it didn't matter how far we drove away they just kept following. Any time we slowed or stopped, they began pecking at the truck, sounding like very large hail stones raining down on us. I was sure they would break a window or at the very least put a dent in the body.

The owner came over, wondering why we were heading in the wrong direction in circles. He chased off the birds long enough for me to quickly open the cover, keeping one nervous eye on the birds and breathing a sigh of relief as I jumped back into safety. He loaded the truck in no time, three buckets of the bobcat, the springs groaning manure overflowing the sides. We gingerly made our way back home. Thank goodness it was only a five-minute drive. Ostrich shit is heavy. Probably aged for at least a year. It had no smell and was the richest, darkest, mature, and well-structured soil we could have wished for. Often fresh manure is too rich to use as soil and needs mixing with other materials, which we didn't have. I was sure this compost would work perfectly well on its own.

There were a lot of projects that had a greater urgency than the garden. Like building the workshop and getting the well hooked up, and the pumphouse built. But it felt satisfying to be working on something nurturing and getting ready to grow things.

Now we had our ostrich manure/soil I was looking for a quick method to get us a garden we could use within the next month. We constructed a 4-foot by 12-foot raised bed, using some of the discarded wood concrete forms. Rather than digging, clearing, and levelling the rough ground, we used cardboard and newspaper to lay a thick layer at the bottom. Then filled the bed with a mixture of manure, and the sandy soil we had close by. This gave us a raised garden about 12 inches deep, all we needed to do now was leave it to settle down and warm up. We could plant around the end of May, which I had calculated to be the approximate last frost date for the area.

I'd also been reading about an old method of gardening called hügelkultur. With all this land, and so much room to put in garden beds, I was in heaven. Previously, I would have been lucky to find a 6-foot square to use or grow everything in pots. Where would we start? So many ideas!

The Wikipedia definition: Hügelkultur, literally mound bed or mound culture, is a horticultural technique where a mound constructed from decaying wood debris and other compostable biomass plant materials is later planted as a raised bed. It struck me as being perfect for our new garden; we had lots of rotting wood, had lots of land to clear, and needed moisture retention. I was keen to try it out. We constructed a small test bed to try it out, using old tree trunks laid lengthways, with newer branches, and leaves, and topped with dug soil.

Chapter Twenty-Eight: Bob the Bobcat

For the next few days, we cleared the wooden formwork still strewn around the concrete pad and filled in the excavations around the edges. This was back-breaking work, with hand shovels, rakes, and wheelbarrows. The round river boulders, about the size of a soccer ball and smaller, were very dense heavy granite, way heavier than they looked. It was all we could do to roll them to the side. Most of the time, it was too hard to kick the shovel into the pile to pick up dirt and awfully slow going. But slowly, we transformed and levelled the area and removed the treacherous trenches around the pad. With crushed rock left over from the foundation, we built a ramp to reverse the trailer up onto the pad. We neatly stacked all the wooden formwork to the side, and we had a new home for the trailer.

One more task to perform before moving the trailer. We had noticed a fairly big dead tree leaning toward the workshop site, which would need to come down before putting the trailer in its path. Dave fired up the chainsaw and soon had the tree down. It was hollow inside and full of ants. We bucked and stacked the logs nearby to give the ants time to move, as we wanted the logs for the newly dug firepit.

Parking the trailer on the pad would give us a perfectly level clean campsite until construction of the workshop later in the year. Moving the trailer was straightforward enough, even though it was a tight spot to reverse into. My reversing skills were definitely improving. It felt much nicer to be camping back at the primary site rather than like squatters on the side of the driveway.

Once in position, we now had plenty of clean space to put out the trailer awning, set out of chairs, and cook on the temporary fire pit.

We discussed our next purchase by the fire after dinner, after experiencing the hard and slow work of moving the small pile of excavated rocks and dirt by hand. Back on Facebook, we came across a mini excavator for sale just down the road. It was older, but at a price we could afford. We'd been exploring the idea of a mini tractor with a backhoe, front loader, and other implements, but that would be a major expense that was hard to justify. This older machine might need maintenance, but was more suited to the type of work we were lining up. Digging trenches for the water pipes and cables, levelling the driveway. We could pay someone to do the work, which would be quicker, but then we would have to rely on their availability. Or spend the money on equipment, spend the time learning how to operate it, and be independent. Plus, once all the work was complete, we would still have the excavator to sell if we wanted to.

After viewing the mini-bobcat excavator having a quick tryout of the machine, and I have to admit; having very little idea of what we were examining; we agreed on a price. Which was probably not the best decision we have made, but we did it and would pick it up on our next trip in May. We were now the proud owners of Bob the Bobcat. No more hand shoveling for us!

With all our major goals for the trip completed and a couple of days to spare, we could turn our attention to more housekeeping tasks.

The workshop area was still in disarray, with piles of dirt and jumbled rocks, despite our efforts to even out the ground near the concrete pad. In time, nature would transform the bare earth with new grasses and shrubs growing through. There wasn't much else we could do until the Bobcat arrived. However, the surrounding wild forest was a tempting, unkempt blank canvas waiting to be transformed.

In early spring the undergrowth was grey and dead looking, a few sparse ground-hugging prickly mahonia's, their dark green leaves the only colour. The bright green fiddleheads of the bracken still sleeping curled underground. They had logged the forest many years ago. We could see the rotted stumps of large trees and the scars across the ground from heavy equipment. The forest has done its best to hide the damage and repair itself with hundreds of new saplings and many trees growing close together. All the fresh growth competing for light and moisture. Forests left to their own devices will self-manage and we could already see the results of this. Weak spindly trees either dead and leaning against each other or younger trees sapping the energy and killing larger trees.

We planned to thin out the trees, keeping the largest and healthiest specimens, and open up the ground below to encourage shrubs, grasses, and wildflowers. Cut off the lower dead branches of the evergreens to remove the fuel in case of wildfires. We started with removing the dead trees, limbing, and bucking those big enough for firewood. Huge piles of tree limbs and brush accumulated that we weren't sure what to do with. If we had had a chipper, it would have been perfect to chip and spread the material as a mulch between the trees. But for now, we were just satisfied with clearing out and storing the brush in piles. Perhaps it would be good for the hügelkultur beds at some point.

We wanted to leave as many trees as possible, in natural random order, and give them a better chance of survival. Very satisfying work, like painting a picture, taking time to stand back and look from a variety of angles to see which trees had well-balanced groupings. It crossed my mind it would take us years to complete the whole five acres.

That Easter, the small patch we completed, looked so much better. By opening up the view between the trunks and clearing all the dead, it just felt more alive and healthy. Even though the days were warm enough for no jackets, the evenings were chilly. It was our routine to light the fire, for cooking and then warmth into the evening while admiring our day's work.

Our last task for this trip was to tidy up the pathway to the outhouse. Deep ruts and drag marks scarred most of the five acres, hidden below the shrubbery, waiting to trip at every step. Blake had made a path to the outhouse with his backhoe, but it was bumpy and a hazard in the dark. We had about seven tonnes of washed gravel left over from the workshop foundation, which was a perfect pathway material. I explained my plan to Dave, to take a few wheelbarrows full and spread them with the rake to fill in the low spots and make an easy trail to the outhouse. We stood back to admire our efforts. It certainly looked a lot better, but still didn't quite look finished. It needed some defining feature, something to demarcate the edges. With a flash of inspiration, I loaded the wheelbarrow with some round boulders and rocks that we had separated from the excavations. We were keeping them separate for a future project we had in mind to build a stone fireplace, oven, and chimney for the outdoor kitchen. There was no shortage, and the smaller rocks would be perfect as an edging for the outhouse path. That was what it needed. We scattered wildflower seeds on either side of the path, in the hope some would win against the natural undergrowth, and add a splash of colour later in the year.

The indigenous forest was naturally beautiful, with at least 15 different tree species. We wanted to add more diversity by adding flowers and shrubs, to attract butterflies, bees, and birds. All too soon, it was time to load the truck, close up the trailer, and head back to reality, work, and life. I was already planning our next trip. But it would have to wait longer than expected. They moved my gran to another hospital because her condition worsened. Her health was deteriorating and on top of that, she had COVID. I headed back to England again to spend time with her. Most of the time spent keeping her company by her bedside, it was heartbreaking to see this once strong and vibrant lady, so frail and weak, struggling for breath. At time she was like her old self and we would chat about people and old times, and at other moments just content to hold her hand while she slept. She was determined and struggled through, and day by day came back to us.

Chapter Twenty-Nine: Pumphouse Planning

Our time back at home was not idle. There were many challenges and problems to put our mental energy into solving. After staying on the land in the trailer for a few days at a time, there were a few creature comforts we were keen to address. Access to a water source, access to a power source, having heating to stay warm, and handling black water waste. We wanted to be self-sufficient and not need to go off site for any of these everyday items. Things that at home we took for granted.

So far, we had checked off the wastewater handling by building the outhouse.

To get water, required power, and came down to two key decisions. What would we use as our source of power? What type of well pump setup did we need?

We had access to a power line at the back of the property, so could hook up the BC Hydro, or we could invest in a solar power system. Either way would be a major expense and would take time to build the infrastructure. As a temporary option, we purchased an inverter generator as a good short-term investment. Portable power, to run tools, the well pump, and power the trailer if needed. Would be a good backup to whatever permanent power solution we decided upon later.

Whatever permanent power solution we opted for, we still needed a structure to house the well pump, hook up to power, and securely store tools and equipment. We were rapidly outgrowing the outhouse as a storage building. We needed to build a pumphouse, which would also double up as storage for the generator and chainsaw. Encouraged by our success with the outhouse, we were confident. After all, it was only slightly bigger. We had downloaded a set of plans for an 8-foot by 8-foot shed that would be big enough for the well-pump equipment. But not too big, as it would need to be heated during the winter to stop the pump from freezing. There was enough lumber from the workshop formwork and free wood we'd repurposed from job sites, to make it relatively economic to build. All we needed was to purchase a few sheets of plywood and the metal roofing material to finish it.

At that point, we were almost certain we would opt to go on-grid for power. It seemed logical, as we were lucky enough to have the power pole right at the property line. If we built the pumphouse directly over the well, it was close enough to run the power line straight to the pumphouse with no extra pole.

When planning each building project, it always seemed more simple initially thinking about it than it ended up being in practical terms. We had the blueprint plans for the pumphouse, and most of the building materials, and I was keen to jump in and get started. But it became apparent that several steps needed completion before we could start building. The water pipe from the pump to the workshop and cabin needed to be buried to protect it from freezing. This meant the excavation needed to be dug out, pipe laid, and filled in before putting the pumphouse on top. Then the section of pipe between the ground and the floor of the pumphouse needed heavy insulation to prevent freezing. As we were using concrete pier blocks as the foundation to support the frame, instead of pouring a concrete pad, which we felt was simpler and less work. Plus more movable in the future if we made any mistakes.

Now into May and better weather, it was perfect timing to get started on the pumphouse project. We estimated a week to build the pumphouse, excavating, burying pipe, framing, and roofing. This would also include learning how to operate the Bobcat.

This was fairly ambitious given our lack of experience and caused a few heated debates between Dave and me. I was probably overconfident and certainly determined to get it done. Dave was less motivated and more interested in exploring the area, taking long lunch breaks, and having a few beers. I was not very good at remembering this was mostly my dream and while Dave was supportive to a point; he did not share my level of enthusiasm for working from first light until we could no longer see what we were doing. We had quite different perspectives. I wanted to work hard and as long to get everything finished so we could relax afterward knowing the job was done. Dave's view was that no matter how hard we worked, I would always find another job I wanted to get done. He wanted to pace himself and fit in leisure activities, even though the project was incomplete. This was so hard for me to comprehend. Coming from a very strong 'work comes first' ethic from growing up on a farm in England. I just could not relax or imagine stopping work to go to the lake when there was still so much to do. It was causing big arguments between us. We had so little time and could not afford to waste it at the lake was how I saw it. But if we were ever to enjoy our time there and not begin hating it, I would have to be prepared to compromise. To give Dave some of what he wanted or he would soon go on strike and refuse to help at all. I could not do it without his help. We intended this to be a place we could come to relax, enjoy being outside and get away, but our differences were getting in the way. I felt resentful that he was jeopardizing our efforts to make progress by constantly wanting to stop work. When all I focused on was just getting the next bit finished. My dad was skilled with building and fixing things and had so much general knowledge about tools, construction, and operating machinery. I was unaware of the amount of knowledge I had gained, some intentionally taught by him and some just from watching him work. Dave was a city boy, but loved spending time outside hiking, fishing, and skiing when he could. It was just so different from my outdoor country experiences. We had quite different skills. What Dave lacked in practical skills, he made up for in his willingness to learn and give things a go. We may have had some intense moments, but once over our differences, we could work well together.

I must mention the personal, and relationship challenges we encountered in developing the land. It was not all sugar-coated. There were major arguments, and we needed time apart to cool down many times.

Chapter Thirty: Bob gets to Work

We had arranged to pick up the Bobcat as the first task of our next stay. We didn't have a trailer or means of getting the excavator, so Blake kindly offered to help us out again. It was a beautiful sunny spring as we headed over to the farm to transfer the money and pick up Bob, as we had so originally named our mini excavator. Blake skillfully maneuvered the tracked excavator up the ramps. Thank goodness, because it was not anything Dave or I could have attempted, having never actually driven or operated an excavator before. Perhaps this had not been such a great idea. A niggling doubt tickled the back of my mind, but I put it aside. Too late now. We just better learn how to operate it.

Blake gave us a crash course in maintenance once we got back home before offloading the machine.

"Have you got a grease gun?" he asked

"No" I felt foolish. It seemed obvious now that we should have one.

"Have you got hydraulic oil?"

"No,"

"Have you got the manual, so we can check what oil it needs?"

"Uh no" Jeez, what had we done? All the money we had invested into this piece of equipment, we were completely incompetent in knowing how to look after it.

After giving the machine a once over, he established the drive motor seal on one track had failed after filling it with oil that promptly ran out all over the bed of the trailer. We would have a major repair into the future but could manage for now. This was a bit of a blow, but had committed to taking care of Bob and determined to download the manual and learn all we could about looking after him. All greased up, fluids topped up, we had work to do. The battery was old as they had not used the machine much for a few years, but there was enough life to get him started. I jumped into the seat and tracked on over to the pumphouse site, to start the first task of digging the trench for the water pipe.

It was surprisingly easy and, to my great relief, not too difficult to operate. I'm not saying I was a natural or very efficient initially, but I could get a reasonable bucketful of soil within a few shaky tries. A little jerky to start with. It took a bit of time to remember which direction the bucket was going to move in. But in no time at all, Bob was eating through the earth and a decent size hole opened up beneath us. The power in even such a small machine compared to using a hand shovel was just mind-boggling. Relaxing, I got the rhythm of extending the arm, lowering the bucket, and pulling back while feathering the bucket. We finished the excavation and placed the first section of pipe.

It was a different story with filling the trench. I just could not get the hang of getting the pile of earth back into the hole. I'm sure any experienced operator would have lots of tips to explain how to do this. However, I positioned the bucket and the machine; it was a pathetic attempt, and I was very glad there was only Dave to witness it. I tried pushing soil in with the blade on the front and tried dragging the earth with the bucket, but nothing was very successful. Thank goodness it was only a small section to fill at this point. We finished it, but it was very frustrating. Hopefully, I could improve with experience for the full 200-meter stretch of trenching.

I was very relieved to give Bob a rest and move on to the pumphouse build and leave the machine operation behind for the day.

Chapter Thirty-One: Pumphouse Build

We estimated the building materials for the pumphouse, had 2 x4s on hand, and had leftover wood from the workshop for the floor. Blake's home-milled wood was thicker than dimensional lumber. We had perfect bright spring weather to get started. Jackets soon shed in the warm sunshine. It felt like we were in another world, away from winter back in Canmore, birds singing in the gentle breeze. Shimmering bright green leaves and sticky balsam poplar buds giving off a beautiful aroma of honey and caramel.

We quickly accomplished the next stage, screwing the floor joists together and levelling the floor on concrete piers. We positioned the floor framework so the well casing was in the building's corner, giving us maximum space without the well being in the way. Our calculations and measurements put us well within the required maximum distance from the electric pole. So when we came to hook up to power, the power company could run the line straight from the main pole to the corner of the pump house. A transformer is required to step down the power running through the main line. Luckily for us, there was a transformer already installed, so it would be less expensive to get connected.

By following our free internet shed plans, we constructed the framing for the four walls on the ground. We had a range of battery-operated power tools, drill, circular saw, and jigsaw. But soon discovered the circular saw didn't quite have the power to cut effectively. So this gave us a chance to try out the new generator and use the bigger circular saw, which was much smoother. We were feeling proud of our accomplishment. We had all the tools, materials, and resources, and would soon have somewhere secure and weatherproof to store everything. Each minor success was one step closer to making life more comfortable. Constructing the wall frames on the ground was difficult, having to adjust to make everything straight on the uneven terrain. It was simple enough for the two of us to carry the eight feet walls into place and hold steady while screwing down some temporary support. It was looking like a proper building.

We put together leftover plywood pieces to cover the walls and give them strength. Ever conscious of Dave's tolerance of manual labour for the day, it was a good point to stop. We were on schedule and as long as we completed the structure and made it watertight before leaving, we would be happy. As we sat by the trailer in the afternoon sun, the thermometer topped 20C, yet again BC weather was kind to us.

Day two–we moved on to the roof rafters. These all needed to be cut at an angle and constructed individually. This took some figuring out, but once we had the first put together we had a template for the rest. When the spring weather changed to showers, we worked on the roof trusses under the trailer canopy, using the tailgate of the truck as a workbench.

With such a small footprint, it didn't take long to get the roof trusses secured into place. I climbed up on top; the trusses held! A good start. With another of Dave's purchases, we cut the metal roof panels down to size and secured them in place. Before the day was done, we had a roof! I couldn't wait for another rainstorm to check out the waterproofing. The door was still to be completed, but most of the work was done, and we had a dry place to keep all our tools safe and sound in-between visits.

Chapter Thirty-Two: New Name & Gold Claim

Since we had found the land in BC, we had always resorted to just calling it "the land". In the beginning, it had been more because we did not want to tempt fate and presume it would end up becoming ours. We couldn't call it 'home' as we didn't live here enough, and it was only raw land. Because of its proximity, we often said we were going to Edgewood.

We wanted a name, something to define what it meant to us, but not to be too silly. With a blank canvas, we had gone through a few candidates and tried them out for a while, but they didn't feel just right. I liked Fernthwaite, a combination of the old English word "thwaite" and the beautiful ferns growing in large quantities under the shady trees. The meaning of Thwaite is a piece of land used as a meadow, field, or pasture; specifically, forestland cleared and converted to tillage. It certainly fit well in terms of meaning, but didn't exactly roll off the tongue. We'd be forever spelling it to everyone else. Common terms such as Birchwood and Fernwood, for obvious reasons, worked well but were not unique enough. We were fortunate with the weather while pouring the concrete for the workshop foundation, it was a sheltered spot - a little "haven". Peaceful, warm, and sunny, sheltered with little wind. When we retreated into our little haven, the rest of the world faded away. "Fernhaven", we liked it, it felt right. We'd try it out, see how it sounded, and hopefully, it would stick. So the land became Fernhaven.

Since the pump house build was progressing so well, and we were well on our way to completion, it was time to give in to Dave's desire for exploring. During our research phase a year ago, we stumbled across someone selling a gold claim in the area. This appealed to our sense of adventure. Imagine finding gold. Maybe we could finance building a cabin if we struck it lucky! We got gold fever! After more research, we realized it wasn't hard to get a free miner certificate and register our placer gold claim rather than buy one from someone else. Barnes Creek, a 30-minute drive, already had several registered claims on it. Although we knew nothing about the lay of the land or what would make a suitable location for finding gold, we registered a claim, just for fun. Panning for gold might be fun for a day off from developing the land. With the help of GPS coordinates and google earth, we had pinpointed a suitable grid that was not already claimed. We could see the access might be challenging as it was a very steep descent to the creek from the forestry road. Perhaps that would make it a worthwhile spot to speculate. That had been back in the winter. Now it was time to venture up the forestry road and try to find our claim. Given the recent weather and the fact there was no snow at all left on the ground, we thought it an ideal time to go try our luck.

After leaving the main paved highway and following the forestry road for 15 km, we no longer had cell signal and started going up. With Barnes Creek on our right, we wound our way slowly up the bumpy track. Patches of wet snow were still visible under the dense canopy of dark cedars, dropping away alarmingly. Down to what we guessed would be the creek far below, even though there was no chance of seeing it through the thick tangled mess of trees. We had marked GPS on google earth and slowed as we got close to the spot where we expected the claim to be. Even though well maintained, three feet to the right of the gravel road was an almost vertical drop towards the creek. From the map, we had calculated it to be about half a kilometre from the road, but had not counted on that being a vertical half kilometre. We were 3000 feet higher than Fernhaven and it showed the temperature was 15C cooler, and the snow was still thick under the trees without warmth or sunlight to melt it away. Even though we were confident we had the right spot, it would have to wait until our next trip. Before we could attempt to climb down, given the depth of snow and a dense tangle of downed trees, to clamber over.

Back to Fernhaven and we were never in need of things to do. Our small garden created with ostrich manure on the last trip was ready for planting. We were working on a last frost date of May 24th, which was like Canmore, but the growing season extended longer here, with hotter days over the summer. As we still had no water or options to irrigate, planting now to take advantage of the early spring weather, we hoped we might get lucky. It would be trial and error. Potatoes, beets, green beans, and swiss chard were on the menu, for our first attempt. The black earth was warm, damp, and easy to work. Little rough seeds lovingly dropped into tiny holes. Potato chips with green eyes sprouting banked up. All would have to take their chances without our constant attention. Protected by a roll of fencing we picked up at the local community garage sale, would help to keep out any speculative deer looking for tender greens.

We were constantly balancing work to earn money to pay for the next building materials and having to be back in Canmore. I had the potential to work remotely at Fernhaven, but the internet was slow having to hotspot from my cell phone. It was distracting trying to work in the trailer when there were always so many more interesting things to do on the property. I resented any time clients called or when I needed to sit in front of my computer working. Plus, we had such limited time and always a long list of tasks to finish. Most of them needed to be completed before we had to pack up and go home.

Dave and I were having many debates about how much money we would need to develop the property. Dave wanted to borrow more money to complete the project, including getting power and water and building the cabin. I did not want to take on more debt. I didn't want to be tied to working to earn money all the time and not have enough free time to spend at Fernhaven. Because Dave is older, I wanted to be sure we were not so committed to working for the rest of our lives that we would never have time to enjoy spending time there. We also had different long-term goals. This had never been on Dave's wish list to buy and develop the land. He was happy in Canmore, working, playing golf, hiking in the summer, and skiing in the winter with a winter sun holiday. It was not his desire to live full time at Fernhaven; he worried about what we would do all winter. At this point in the project, I was reserving judgment, as I did not know what I wanted long term. I loved being at Fernhaven, the potential, and space to potter about in the trees. But once we had finished all the building, would I still enjoy being there so much? I wanted to try it out and see. I believed Dave would enjoy the freedom and find more projects to keep him interested and busy if we were there for longer periods. But knew that he would have to come to that decision himself. All I could do was provide opportunities for him to make up his mind. We were still a long way from having the facilities to stay long term, so had to be content with short bursts of hard work, and then prepare for the next trip. Sometimes it was hard to see all we had accomplished in the short few days we were there and too easy to just see how much more there was to do. In the six days we had been here this time, we had built the pumphouse, planted the garden, and learned how to operate the Bobcat. We drove away, with heavy hearts already thinking about what we would do next time.

Cell service is patchy for much of the journey through BC until we get closer to home. There are small windows where messages might get through, just off the ferry and just around Nakusp. I had seen a missed call on WhatsApp from my mum but not been able to get enough signal to return the call. Then for a moment got signal and my dad called.

"We're driving home, so I won't have a signal for long," I warned him.

"Oh I see, well I…." he disappeared. Signal had dropped again.

Five kilometres further and a message popped up from my dad. My gran had passed away. It was a very sad, silent trip home. I felt numb, tears running down my face. She had been my inspiration, the matriarch of our family, so kind, loving and strong. Now she was gone. The glue that held our family together. What would we do without her?

I travelled back to England for the third time in as many months for her funeral. It was not how we had planned to spend the first few months of this year. Causing a lot of disruptions being away from home and work. But I was so very grateful for the time I had had with gran, even though it was not where she had wanted to be at the end. God bless you gran, if I could be even a tiny part like you, I would be happy.

Chapter Thirty-Three: Getting Water

Last year's rush to create the concrete foundation was over, and the trailer had survived the winter, so there was less urgency to build the workshop. After all, the workshop was mainly to protect the trailer from snow load, and not needed until next wintertime. The build was frequently on my mind, wondering how we would get it built if we could find any help, and how difficult it would be. I was happy to put that problem aside for a while and focus on other creature comforts. For our seven day stay in June, getting water was our next project. We now turned our attention to the well. Knowing exactly nothing about wells, pumping water, water quality, etc. it was hard to know where to start.

We asked around a few of our plumbing contacts, but none of them had any experience with wells. Getting a contractor to come out and look was going to cost several thousand dollars we didn't have, so it was down to us to work out a solution. What would we do without Google and YouTube?

It is a shallow well at 25 feet, and with much research and googling, we opted for a jet pump with a small pressure tank. It might not be suitable for the eventual total water requirements for the cabin, but it would do for now. Especially when there was just such a pump at half-price at

Canadian Tire. The well was about 200 feet distance from the workshop. The water line would eventually need to be buried at least three feet underground to protect against freezing.

Plumbing pipe connectors and fittings are the most confusing things in the world. I have a lot more admiration for plumbers after trying to work out how to connect the downpipe, the foot valve, go from 1 ¼ inch to 1inch pipe, adding shut-off and drain valves. When we had finally come up with what we thought was a reasonable setup, trying to get the parts we needed was frustrating. We spent many hours in various stores trying to find the right parts, even online. If you don't know the names of everything male and female, adaptors, and connectors, it's a baffling minefield. We needed to prepare and bring all parts with us to the site as it was too far to discover we were missing a $2 part. However, the well stocked local village store had a surprising array of parts you would never expect to find.

Our initial idea was to use the generator to power the well pump. We could turn it on for brief periods to pump up enough water to use for the garden and our personal use while we were there. We knew there was water in the well but had not sampled it to see what the quality was like. Our neighbours assured us the water was good quality and plenty of it. They had been using it for years.

The foot valve at the bottom of the well to filter any particles connected to the downpipe that hooked into the pump. The pump has a pressure switch that, when the tank fills up to pressure, switched off the pump. From the tank, we had the 200 feet of 1-inch pipe. We temporarily ran overground to the trailer parked at the workshop. I put a ball valve in place at the pump to allow water to be drawn off if needed. We measured all the lengths of the poly pipe, heated the pipe to soften it, and connected all the parts with push connectors and hose clamps. It all seemed tight and secure. Now, for the moment of truth, would it work? With the generator fired up, we plugged in the pump. The generator certainly kicked up a notch, so something was pulling power and the pump seemed to work, but we couldn't tell what it was doing. The pressure gauge needle trembled but didn't move. Voice raised over the generator noise, Dave asked, "is it doing anything?" I shrugged. We were both newbies and were not sure how long it would take. The pump instructions had said it didn't need priming, but maybe it did. We shut everything down, feeling very disheartened. What would we do if we couldn't figure it out? Once again, our lack of knowledge and experience was frustrating.

"OK, let's think this through," I said, more to myself. "Maybe the pump needs priming to get it started."

We removed the pressure switch on top of the pump housing and poured in some water until it overflowed. Once again, we started everything back up. The generator sped up as the pump started. Again, the pressure gauge needle vibrated like it wanted to move, but stayed at zero. I looked at Dave, and as I reached over to pull the plug, the pump clunked and we heard gurgling at the bottom of the well casing. The pressure gauge started climbing.

"It's pumping something now!" I grinned. "Bloody hell, we did it! We actually made it all work,"

As the needle reached the high-pressure mark, the pump shut off. I turned off the generator to save shouting over the noise. I grabbed the water bottle and opened the valve. Air sputtering, at first we soon had a steady stream of crystal clear water quickly filling the bottle. It was one of the most satisfying sights we had achieved so far. We had water. Just to be sure there was enough pressure throughout the system, Dave walked back to the trailer and opened the valve at the end of the 200-foot hose. He filled our 20-litre container and hooked up the garden hose to water the garden. We achieved another step toward independent living.

In the month since we planted the garden, the BC weather benefited us. Cooler than usual and with more rain, our garden flourished. Everything was growing rich lush healthy plants. It was amazing to see how big everything had gotten in that brief time. But now the BC summer had really heated up, and I wasn't so sure the garden would keep going without help. Now we had water we could at least keep the garden watered while we were there, and hope there would be enough showers to keep the plants healthy until our next trip.

Chapter Thirty-Four: Summer Camp Plans

The well pump setup was not ideal, but would get us through for now. To get water, we had to go start the generator, switch on the pump, fill our containers, then switch off the pump once the well ran dry. Then wait until the well replenished before completing the process. We had been dipping the well depth every half an hour to see how quickly it was refilling. With only a 6-inch well casing, at nine feet of water, there was not much of a reservoir to pump from. As the well was unused since being drilled at least seven years previously, we were hoping continual use would help to increase the flow. We could shock the well and clean it out. Options for the future, but we'd use it as it was for now, and deal with that challenge when we had the capacity and know-how.

It always felt as we took each step forward, we discovered a fresh problem that we had not even known we would have to overcome. These new challenges became obvious once we were at that point, but previously we'd been blissfully unaware. Perhaps it's a good thing, as knowing everything at the starting point may have been so overwhelming we may not have even wanted to get started.

I remembered reading about the four stages of competence, especially since our land purchase.

In the beginning, we are unconsciously incompetent, meaning we are not aware of what we don't know. Then we become consciously incompetent, we realize what we don't know, just still can't do it well. Through practice and learning, we can reach conscious competence. But it takes an enormous effort and time to be sure to do things competently. Then finally unconscious competence, where we don't have to think and are just able to do things competently. At every step of this project, we were fluctuating between stages one and two. With perhaps brief moments of stage three, it was exhausting! I couldn't even contemplate the future once we were into more complex work, like building the workshop, or a cabin, what this would mean. I guess the one consolation was that we were getting used to the feeling and could expect that the unexpected would happen all the time.

Temperatures soared to the high twenties, and flowers bloomed. Bright red poppies, purple lupins swaying in the breeze, visited by happy busy bees. You'd have thought we planned the area and cultivated the flower borders. But we could not claim any part in this beautiful display mother nature had taken over and shown us her best. A sense of pride swelled at every visit to the outhouse, to see the small building we had built with our own hands. The path carefully formed by stones dug and hauled by our efforts and now bordered by colourful flowers and greenery. Those small successes and visual delights made the work all so worthwhile.

The black 200-foot water pipe snaking through the undergrowth from the pumphouse was getting enough sun to absorb a lot of heat. Enough so we could take a hot shower right from the faucet. We took turns to hold the thick heavy pipe for each other, a quick strip down on the hot concrete. Working quickly to make sure there was sufficient hot water and pressure in the line for us both to get equal time under the water. Hoping none of our neighbours would show up for a visit, as we hopped around naked under the too hot water. A welcome hose down at the end of each sweaty day of hard labour. We were still levelling the ground around the concrete foundation to give us the space to erect the steel arches of the workshop.

This brought us back to tackle the shortcut trailer winterization we'd performed back in October of the year before. We needed to get rid of the pink liquid not only in the trailer water lines but also in the freshwater tank. We could not rely on enough supply or water and pressure to rinse out the tank from the intermittent supply from the well. I booked a couple of nights at a campground in Burton across the ferry. With a full hookup campsite, it would give us a chance to flush out the water tanks, empty the black water tanks, and spring clean the trailer. Burton City cider was a short walk away and, being on the lake shoreline, we could get the paddleboards in the water. It would feel like a holiday! Without having to take the trailer too far.

It was a luxury, having both full power and water hookup. We could use the microwave, TV, and shower in the trailer. We could lie in bed in the morning looking out at the lake, and have a leisurely breakfast. Spending the afternoon stand-up paddling on Arrow Lakes, stopping for cider refreshments. It was a well-earned brief interlude, but chores were calling and we had another project with a deadline to get back for.

Even though the workshop erection was still in the future, we needed to move the trailer off the concrete pad to make space for the building. We had been looking around for a pleasant spot to move to during the summer. Somewhere close enough to the outhouse, with delicate shade for the trailer but sunny enough for morning coffee. A level spot that we could get in and out of without too much trouble. We had five acres, which posed more of a challenge through the number of choices. We wanted it far enough away that we weren't constantly looking at the workshop construction site.

There was a suitable spot, through a small, wooded patch directly opposite the workshop. It opened out into a grassy clearing sheltered by a couple of large ponderosa pines. The access would mean cutting a few spindly conifers and putting Bob to work, digging out the tree roots and spreading some washed gravel for a driveway. The grass area was mostly level, with only minor excavation needed to fill the ruts from past logging. We planned to minimize the amount of change to the area so that in the future the land would return to its natural state, in case the summer camp might be only temporary. I marked out an s-shaped driveway through the trees to leave the largest, healthiest spruce and cedar trees and help the access look more natural. Dave's chainsaw roaring soon had the few small trees down on the ground and began the laborious task of limbing them up. We were going to keep the trunks whole for potential poles and construction in the future. We had a good routine for tree and brush clearing. Dave, having more experience on the chainsaw, would fell the trees I pointed out, then I'd drag them to a suitable spot to limb-up. With heavy boots, chainsaw helmet, face shield, earmuffs, and chaps it was hot, heavy work wading in amongst the undergrowth. As Dave cut away the brush, I would clear away and drag all the branches and pile them up off to the side. It is amazing how much brush there is from even a few small trees. We had accumulated four large piles that, at this point in the year, could do nothing with. We'd wait until winter to burn up the waste, so as not to leave it as fuel for forest fires. The future option that I much preferred was to buy a wood chipper to mulch down all the waste. We could either keep for pathways, compost it or just spread it under the trees to return it to the forest.

The tree-clearing work was a task for early mornings as by mid-morning and onwards, it was far too hot to be sweating in the noise and fumes of the chainsaw.

Whatshan Lake was a pleasurable distraction for the afternoons. It was much warmer than the larger Arrow Lake, with a small beach and floating dock offshore. A favourite with locals, but off the beaten track, bumping over the rutted forest road to get there, was worth the effort to slide into the cool, refreshing water.

Chapter Thirty-Five: Stump Pulling

With the trees gone and the winding new driveway opened up, Dave had his doubts that we could get the trailer through. He wanted to take out another tree. There were two that crowded in quite close to the new trail, but they were such healthy tall trees and offset from each other, I was sure we could wiggle through. Their position screened the workshop construction zone from our new summer camp nicely, so we elected to leave them for now. After all, once we cut them down, we could not put them back.

Time to get Bob into action, to level out the ruts, and dig out the four stumps that were directly in the pathway. Both novices and very inexperienced with excavator operation and care, we called in a local mechanic. To give the excavator a full service and change the filters, hydraulic oil, and engine oil. We were unaware of the last time someone had fully serviced the Bobcat. The previous owner seemed less experienced than us and we had some doubts about how much regular maintenance had been done. We had already replaced the battery, which wasn't a surprise. After the service, Bob started smoothly and seemed to run well. With hindsight, we probably should have left a longer length on the stumps. We could have either pushed them over with the excavator pulling the whole stump out in one go or at least had more leverage with the bucket. As it was, we needed to excavate quite a big hole around each root, pulling out boulders and smaller roots until locating the large taproot. It was unbelievable how tough those roots were, making the bobcat work hard. I am sure it could easily have pulled the machine over before the root gave up. Once we had the spidery ball of roots, dirt, and rocks loose, it was a case of shaking off all the excess soil and sand. Then placing them to one side, another pile growing to get rid of at some future point. We pushed all the loose material back into the holes made. It took several hours to extract the four large stumps, and we moved on to the grassy area.

The new driveway faced south, and after 200 feet through the wooded area, it opened up to a circular grassy meadow. Three larger pines to the left grouped around a spot that would be ideal for reversing the trailer into. By driving in, towing the trailer, and turning right to straighten up, I could reverse back between the trees, and the door would face the driveway. Being under the large ponderosa pine would give us vital shade during the heat of the day. There would be room to extend the awning to shelter from the rain. From our walk around and survey of the ground, we noticed some over grown ruts. These would need to be levelled with the excavator before attempting the move.

Dave went to get Bob warmed up and ready for the day's work. I was already thinking ahead to finish the driveway with some of the leftover crushed gravel from the workshop foundation. Making a smooth driveway to move into summer camp. We only had a few days to get this last task complete, as we had friends coming to visit with their trailer. They could park on the concrete pad and afterwards it would be clear to start the workshop build.

Suddenly, there was the most horrendous screeching and whining noise coming from Bob. I hardly had time to wonder what had happened before there was a loud bang and then silence. I ran over to Dave and asked. "What on earth was that?"

"I have no idea. I was just trying to start Bob, and it started making a terrible noise, and I shut it off."

As I walked over, it was clear something major had happened. We tried to start the excavator again, but all we could hear was a faint clicking sound, and the engine did not turn over, let alone fire up. It was no good Bob was dead. After calling our mechanic on the phone, he promised to be there first thing in the morning to investigate.

That certainly was a setback. The ground was in no condition to try moving the trailer without work. Even if it had been level enough, the excavator was now broken down in the middle of the new driveway. Not wanting to waste our time, we tried to complete as much as we could by hand. With the pick axe to cut the turf from the ruts, we made some progress. It certainly made us appreciate the power and speed of using the excavator while it lasted. After doing what we could in the grassy area, we took turns filling the wheelbarrow and raking the crushed rock into the craters left by the stumps. As the afternoon wore on and the driveway was sweltering in full sun, even my work ethic and enthusiasm were melting away. This was like a hard labour camp. Bob silently sadly watched from his abandoned spot. It was lake time.

Chapter Thirty-Six: Bob's Diagnosis

Given our time pressure to get the trailer moved, I was keen to solve the problem ourselves and get on with work. I called my dad on WhatsApp to explain what had happened. He asked a series of questions and using the phone camera; I showed him various parts of the engine. He established it was most likely the starter motor. This was good to know, but would require either a new part or rewinding the existing motor. Dad guided me into undoing a few bolts to remove the motor to see if it was seized up. We had a few general-purpose tools, but not very suitable for this kind of task. Reluctantly, we resigned ourselves to waiting for the mechanic to arrive.

"What are all those red marks?" Dave asked, looking at my shoulders.

"No idea. They do feel itchy now you come to mention it."

It turned out that while laying in the grass trying to undo the bolts on the starter motor; I had disturbed some kind of biting bugs, mosquitoes, or who knew what. Wouldn't be doing that again without covering up first.

Mid-afternoon, in the heat of the day, the mechanic arrived and confirmed Dad's suspicion that it was most likely the starter motor. He set to removing it, and it was clear to see that there would have been no way we could have done it ourselves with our limited tools. Kevin and Ann popped by to see what we were doing. They kindly offered to drop the starter motor off in Vernon on the way home and bring it back the following weekend. That would save us a long drive, and although a week later, we might still just about have time to get the trailer moved before our friends arrived. The mechanic was available to come back and reinstall. There always seemed to be unanticipated delays and changes to our plans. Would we ever get a project to run smoothly?

Dave had taken on the twice-daily task of watering the garden. So far the early spring wet weather, now sunshine and heat plus the rich fertile ostrich manure compost was doing wonders for the garden. The potatoes, swiss chard, and beans were visibly growing daily. It was still a chore to start the generator, wait for the pump, head over to the garden, spray the garden, and then turn everything off. But I never tired of watching the crystal clear water creating a rainbow over the garden as the sun's rays caught in the mist. At home, turning on the tap and getting water, we took it completely for granted, not even giving it a second thought. But here, we knew how much effort we had put into getting that water out of the ground. The physical exertion and mental challenges we had overcome, and the sense of achievement, was exhilarating. If we could do this, what else could we achieve?

That evening, while walking back to the pumphouse to shut down, I could hear something hissing. I cautiously peered into the vegetation, wondering at the strange sound. I noticed what looked like steam making dewdrops on the leaves. What on earth was it?

With flip flops flapping I waded into the bush, and could see the black water hose buried in the grass had sprung a leak. That seemed weird. The hose had never been driven over or damaged. It seemed odd that it would suddenly develop a leak.

"Dave!" I wondered if he would hear me. "We've got a leak in the water pipe" as I bent down to examine the leak more closely, water spray quickly soaking my t-shirt. I could see two holes side by side in the pipe, about two inches apart.

"What could have caused that?" Dave asked, peering over my shoulder.

"I don't know, maybe a fault in the material," I surmised. I felt around the pipe and noticed another two dents on the underside of the hose.

"Looks like bite marks," Dave frowned.

I laughed, "Come on, be serious."

"Probably a bear. I don't think a skunk could bite through that thick a hose."

It didn't take too long to fix. With a quick run down to the local store for plumbing supplies that would put Home Depot to shame, we cut the pipe and added a join and we were back in business. Wiser into the future, we would have to pay attention and try to get the water line buried as soon as possible.

With a brief trip home for four days, it hardly felt like we were off the road, and we were back again. summer definitely increased the journey time. There were both benefits and disadvantages. We had more daylight and could leave around five am from Canmore, but there was more holiday traffic on the road. It was not so easy to cruise along without getting stuck behind slow trucks, especially through the pass. On the long holiday weekends, timing our arrival to be at the ferry loading dock ten minutes before the ferry left, did not work at all. We needed to be there much earlier, and even then sometimes we would have to wait for a second ferry as the first one was full. That would add at least an hour, but it was such a beautiful stopping point. We often brought beer and hiked to the rocky bluff overlooking the lake. To enjoy the sunshine, and waves lapping at the shore as we waited for the ferry. There was a small campsite on the edge of the lake, with a boat launch that was popular with anglers. If we had time, we could walk along the shoreline, even when it was 30C the water was toe-numbing within seconds. Originally two smaller lakes 14 kilometres apart, Upper Arrow Lake and Lower Arrow Lake. In 1960, the damming of the Columbia River joined the two lakes into the 230km long lake when they created the reservoir. I couldn't imagine how it had looked before this when the water level was 12 meters lower. From our perspective, once we got on the first ferry, it really felt like we were leaving our regular lives behind and beginning a new adventure every time.

For our second trip in July, we had a different set of objectives than usual. I was having to rein in my constant 24/7 work mode to satisfy Dave's needs for more leisurely focused activities. We had some friends coming to visit in their trailer, and I was enjoying the idea of a few days with them. Before their arrival, we still had to get Bob operational, finish the driveway through the summer camp, and get the trailer moved.

Since the summer days were long, we left Canmore after work for an early start the next morning. Kevin had delivered the rebuilt starter motor, and we had scheduled the mechanic for a simple install first thing that morning. Bob roared back into life, sounding healthier than ever. We shared a relieved sigh, no more back-breaking hand shoveling for a bit. After smoothing out the lump and bumps of the grassy summer camp, Bob moved on, shifting gravel into the potholes from the stump removals. Still not fully competent with the excavator, required the rake to finish the surface.

Now would come the stressful part of maneuvering the trailer into the new spot. It is one thing to look at an area rehearsing the line of travel in your mind. Then actually getting the truck and trailer in position and realize it's a lot bigger and longer than it seemed.

Slowly towing the trailer through the s-bend between the trees was encouraging. It was tight, but over-steering gave me the angle to get the trailer around the trees. Then, pulling as close the trees at the far side of the clearing, I turned sharply right over the newly smoothed ruts. Steady as she goes it was still a little bumpy, thank goodness I'd moved all the breakables in the trailer onto the floor. Then the tricky part was to reverse up, with the goal of squeezing the trailer up between the trees. The truck has big mirrors, which helps, but where was Dave? I needed his guidance to tell me if I was on target, or to go left, go right, or straighten up. Could I see him? No, it was getting more and more frustrating. We had already discussed this beforehand as it had been a problem in the past. I appreciated he had no clue about reversing, so did not know how to give instructions. But I'd explained what I hoped to do, and explained what help I needed, where he needed to stand, etc., etc. But what was he doing? Just standing there, watching.

"I can't see your mirrors," he said, as if that was a good reason for not providing any guidance.

"Well, then ef-ing move so you can, Dave," I expressed my frustration.

It was hot, and I was constantly hopping in and out of the truck to see where the trailer was because Dave was nowhere to be seen when I was looking in the mirrors.

"I need you to guide me. I can't see anything back there," I tried patiently, gritting my teeth.

"OK, where should I go?" he asked.

"I can't tell you that from here. Just move so you can see me in the mirror."

We tried again, slowly creeping backward.

"OK, ok that's good," he beckoned me back. "Whoa, whoa, you'll hit the tree!"

"Jeez, Dave, I can't turn on a dime. You'll have to give more advance instructions to turn than just before I hit something." this was certainly an exercise in keeping calm. I was epically failing.

With a lot of manoeuvring and reassessing the angles, we finally got the trailer into the perfect position. The ground under the trees was quite free of grass and level. The gentle shade from the large, majestic ponderosa pines provided a welcome coolness that only trees seem to provide.

We un-hitched and levelled up, extended the trailer awning, and got everything set up again. It felt nice to be surrounded by greenery and shade after looking at the bare earth and scars of our construction. It was midafternoon, and the thick heat of the day slowed us down. We still had plenty of tasks to get ready for our visitors.

Chapter Thirty-Seven: First Visitors

I was nervous. We had grown used to the inconveniences with lack of facilities. No electric hook up and minimal water, and while we had spoken a lot about our adventures to our friends, I was also hoping they would like what we had and see the beauty. It was a long drive towing their trailer from Alberta. They also had a much longer trailer than ours and we waited in trepidation, wondering where they had got to. Our last task was to move a pile of gravel with Bob so they would have more room to manoeuvre and reverse onto the concrete pad of the workshop. I wasn't sure if they would have to reverse the trailer all the way down the drive, or could turnaround. How would they manage without electricity and limited water? The generator, currently stationed at the pumphouse to power the well pump, was available. But it would be a chore to keep moving it via our hand cart the 200 feet over very rough terrain, if they needed power for the trailer.

The mercury was pushing 33C and knowing my friend did not do well in such hot temperatures; I was nervously carrying my phone around, waiting for the call. We had given them directions on location but were planning on meeting them at the entrance. Just to add more excitement, our neighbours had invited us to a party at their house that afternoon. We really wanted to meet them as we had not had the chance before. These were the landowners who had owned our five acres originally. We hoped we would have time to pop over and say hello before Dawn and Paul, our friends, arrived. It wasn't as if we could abandon our friends just as they arrived. Oh, sorry we are off to a party, thanks for coming we'll see you later. I thought it a bit of a cheek to ask them if we could bring our friends to the party, but Dave reasoned it was not a problem, and thank goodness, they agreed. We were planning to walk over together with Kevin and Ann. With impeccable timing, as Kevin called Dave to say they were on their way, Dawn phoned me to say they were off the ferry and not far away. I urged Dave to go on over as it would be rude to be late, and I would help Dawn and Paul set up and we would head over afterwards if they were up for socialising.

By the time Dave had disappeared into the bush to meet Kevin, I was worried Paul would fly by the turning for Fernhaven. Sweat stinging my eyes, I jogged down the driveway to flag them down, quite aware of a throbbing head from dehydration and overheating. As their big white truck and trailer came into view with nervous excitement, I wondered what our first visitors would think. It was a far cry from the luxurious European river cruise we had enjoyed with Paul and Dawn a few years previously. It was not possible to get much further from that than this.

As they pulled in to my waving hat, Dawn rolled down her window and a blast of artic air conditioning wafted out, reminding me how hot it really was out here.

"Welcome! How was the drive?" I asked.

"Very nice. Where the hell are we? This is the middle of nowhere!" Dawn stated. "We wondered when it was ever going to end."

"It is quite the drive."

Keen to get them set up, Dawn and I walked ahead of Paul, driving. "Jeez, it's sweltering hot," Dawn motioned.

I was worried. Her tolerance for heat was not great and it must have been the hottest we had ever had.

As we reached the concrete, I could tell Dawn was just about at her limit from walking down the driveway. Now it was Paul's turn to manoeuvre their long trailer onto the workshop pad, and I was having serious doubts it would be possible.

Dawn was giving directions. Paul was trying his best to navigate piles of brush, rocks, and logs. The atmosphere was getting tense.

"Let's leave Paul to it. I've got just the thing to cool you down," beckoning Dawn over, "come sit in my truck. We've got air con."

I had a cool drink in the trailer, just the thing to give Paul the time to work his magic in getting the trailer positioned.

With Dawn tucked up our truck air conditioning, belting out cold air, I jumped in with two glasses and a bottle of chilled bubbly I'd been saving for just this moment. We watched Paul from our cool spot, sipping bubbly as he changed his wet shirt and stabilized the trailer.

"He's doing quite well," I observed. "Do you think it's time for you to help him yet?"

Dawn took a sip from her glass, the beads of condensation misting the glass.

"In a moment."

"That went down well."

I noticed the bottle was empty, and decide it was time to take over a cool beer for Paul. The heat pressed on us as we headed over to help.

Once set up, and I'd explained the invitation, we headed over to meet Dave and join the party. Partly to socialize, but also a welcome break from the heat of the afternoon.

Paul and Dawn were soon the life and soul of the party, and fitted right in. The hospitality and friendliness of our new neighbours again overwhelmed us. Several drinks later, looking for Dawn, I learnt she had gone with Ann on the quad for a drive about.

It was late into the evening and dark by the time we found our way stumbling back through bushes and stoney tracks to the Fernhaven campsite.

Dave and I bid our visitors good night, and wobbled to the trailer, my head throbbing from too much sun, too much alcohol and not enough water. Oh boy, did I regret that in the morning?

It was strange to be positioned at the summer camp and having visitors; we were used to getting up and planning days filled with work and the next task. This was more of a holiday to wake up, and think about more leisurely activities that our guests would like to do. It stayed swelteringly hot, and by lunchtime we were all ready to head to the lake, drinks, snacks, and sun hats loaded in the truck.

Twenty minutes to either Whatshan Lake or the Edgewood beach, we spent a pleasant few hours sitting in the water, cooling our drinks, and leisurely swims. Checking out the local golf course, winery, and cidery. We hoped it would have cooled off by evening at Fernhaven, but usually the temp rose again when we returned to camp, away from the cooling lake breeze.

The first yellow, tender skinned potatoes dug, and perfectly fresh green beans picked from the garden, we shared meals together. Not only was it far too hot to have a fire, but not wise given the dry hot conditions. After a few drinks and conversation, we were soon yawning and off to bed.

Paul had borrowed a generator, and this allowed Dawn some respite from the late afternoon heat and to cool their trailer down before evening. It was a good job they had brought it, as the heat lingered on into the evening long after the sun had disappeared behind the trees. It was a successful trip, restful for us all after the hard work we had been putting in. Back in Canmore, I had tried to tell them that there were showers at Edgewood in the campground they could use for a donation and we had water. But the reality of driving all that way just to have a shower was not as practical as I had led them to believe. There were some tense moments, but we hope they left with fond memories and got some quality quiet time. Dawn and Paul wanted to know what we were planning to do in the future. It raised some tough questions that we had thought about but not be able to come up with confident answers. What were our long- and short-term plans? Most probably, these were more difficult to answer because my answers were not the same as Dave's. What compromise would we each be prepared to make?

We both agreed that we wanted to build a cabin. But that was about the only common ground.

I wanted to build it with our own sweat equity, paying for materials as we progressed and borrowing as little as possible. The cabin would then allow us to stay for longer periods, over the summer and winter. With a longer term idea, we may live there full time. But this would be a long-term plan because of saving and building. It might take years. That was the only point I felt let my plan down. To be always working and building would mean it prolonged the stress of construction and would leave little time to enjoy our little haven. I didn't want to spend the next five years constructing our dream cabin. Only to realize there was not enough time to enjoy it with Dave because of his age.

Dave's position was different. He reasoned it made more sense to borrow more money to build a cabin and pay to have a contractor do the work. Arguing we did not have the skills or experience to do it ourselves. His ideal situation would be to visit during the summer and stay in Canmore during the winter for skiing. That way we could continue working and earning money to pay for the extra borrowing. He had no plans to move to Fernhaven full time and felt it was too remote and there was not enough to do if we lived there full time.

Chapter Thirty-Eight: Tigger & Tarps

After saying our goodbye to Paul and Dawn, we were in a rare position of having no major projects currently in progress. Yes, the workshop build was looming, but not an immediate concern. What would we do with our last few days?

While completing the daily task of pumping water, we had another surprise visitor. Just as I was closing up the pumphouse, I heard a tiny meow. I searched through the grass behind the pumphouse, and out popped the cutest little tortoiseshell kitten. With orange eyes, and a scattering of ginger, cream, and black markings, she couldn't have been any prettier. Long black whiskers to the left of her nose, white whiskers to the right, and a stripe of ginger running from the top of her head down to her little pink nose. As she was tortoiseshell, I deduced her to be female, as almost all tortoiseshell cats are female. She was young and tiny, fitting into the palms of my hands as I picked her up. She immediately relaxed and began purring as loudly as she could. Given the direction I had seen her come from, it seemed likely she was a kitten from one of Brett and Elaine's cats. I knew they were away at the moment, so she had probably heard Dave and me talking and come over to say hello. She was very comfortable being handled, and I wasn't sure what to do with her. I was heading back to the trailer, and if I left her there she might follow me, and then get lost trying to get back to the farm. I took her back to our trailer for a visit and decided to bring her back later so she could find her way home. She seemed too small to be wandering so far from home, with who knows what predators around at night time. She was content to jump around, pouncing on leaves, and exploring the summer camp.

"Look who I found," I showed her to Dave. "Isn't she the cutest little kitten? We'll have to give her a name."

She reminded me of a kitten I had rescued when working at the vets many years before, a tortoiseshell very similar to her. I had named that one Poppy and thought it would be a good name. Dave didn't like it and suggested Tigger as she was a little like a tiger, so the little tortoiseshell kitten became Tigger for now. At least until she had to go home. We would eventually learn her name was Winnie.

With the trailer established in our new summer camp, it was time to turn it into a more permanent camp site. In the morning the trees partially shaded the area, but by the later afternoon the sun beat down relentlessly, heating the trailer like an oven. We daren't leave butter or even candles out without some type of container, as they were most likely dripping off the table by the afternoon. Trying to do any type of cooking or work inside the trailer left us drenched in sweat in minutes. Even Dave, who loves the sun, took to moving his chair to the shade after noon. The heat seemed to build until a peak about 3pm and then slightly cool into the evening, once the sun dipped behind the trees to the west.

We made use of the large tarp we had used to cover the trailer the previous winter. It was enormous, very heavy, and difficult to handle. The thick material was black on one side and a reflective silver on the other. We hoped having the reflective layer outwards might protect the trailer from some of the heat. Slinging a wire cable between two of the tallest trees on either side of the trailer, we draped the tarp over the wire. Then used tree poles on the corners to prop it up and make a large canopy for shade. This would also give us a larger area around the trailer protected from rain. Rain seemed the last thing that would ever happen, but we could hope.

Manhandling the heavy tarp up the stepladder was the simple part. Tigger, who decided it was much more fun to hang around with us for the afternoon, struggled to climb up the stepladder and wanted to help. She disappeared under the tarp; I was worried about pushing and pulling the tarp I'd knock her off the trailer roof. It was hard keeping an eye on her. But every time I gave her to Dave to put back on the ground, she would immediately clamber meowing up the ladder again. She was just the cutest little thing. Unfolding and crawling underneath the tarp on top of the trailer, I heaved it into position. This proved to be quite challenging. Dave was on the ground, pulling the ropes attached to the corners, with me shouting directions from under the tarp. We eventually had the thing draped over the trailer in the approximate right spot. Using various tree poles saved from our forest clearing, we attached guy ropes and pulled the tarp tight. With a few adjustments, we now had a canopy over both the trailer and our sitting area. It gave the site a more permanent look about it.

"Where's the kitten?" I asked Dave. Looking around, I hadn't seen her in a while.

"Haven't seen her."

Having seen her last when I was on the roof of the trailer, I scrambled up the ladder again to look under the tarp. There she was curled up in a little ball of fluff, in a sunny spot on top of the tarp, with my sweater I'd discarded earlier. She really was the sweetest little kitten. I was trying not to think about keeping her.

It was a little darker inside the trailer, and not as cool as we had hoped. Knowing the tarp protected the trailer from the brutal UV rays and most of the heat was reassuring. We missed looking out at the millions of stars from the bedroom window, though.

As dusk crept up on us, it was time for Tigger to go home. It tempted me to let her stay overnight, but worried about her being so small, she would get used to being there and come over once we had gone home. She was too small to be wandering the forest on her own. We took her back to the edge of Brett and Elaine's property, placed her down by the barn. We jogged back home, hoping she was smart enough to stay at the barn and that her mum would come find her.

Chapter Thirty-Nine: To Build or not to Build

One thing we were both agreed upon is we would very soon have to get organized to erect the steel workshop. The long days of August were ticking by fast. The weather remained in the thirties. We had collected most of the supplies and materials together. I was dreading installing the Hilti bolts that would secure the metal arches to the concrete. Blake and Rick were available for early September. We had ten days allocated, with extra days to stay if needed. Surely we would get it done in that time… wouldn't we?

I studied the instruction booklet over and over, trying to be sure we were fully prepared and understood what we were doing. We borrowed a scaffold platform from some neighbours and had the necessary tools. Ready for the 1000s of bolts, we would need to tighten, all according to the instruction booklet. It seemed straightforward all we had to do was follow the instructions.

During our two week 'break' at home in Canmore, there was plenty to discuss, plan and research. Physically, it was a rest from the usual heavy labour at Fernhaven, but not a complete break. I could not even remember what I filled my leisure or thinking time before the land. Life had become BL and AL "before buying the land" and "after buying the land". My friends were fed-up with hearing about what I was researching or planning to do next. I felt like I had or was becoming a different person.

We received our mortgage renewal letter from the credit union, and this prompted new discussions. If we were renewing, then it might be an opportune time to look at a further increase in funds to finance a cabin? The land may have increased in value, and we could inquire, no harm in asking.

When to build and the means to build a cabin was a topic that was never far from our minds and discussion. It had progressed to if we were going to build, then what type of building or construction and what size would we want. To distract myself from worrying about workshop construction, I began researching online. I was a member of a couple of "off-grid" groups on Facebook, which always had information about every topic imaginable. If you could sift out the opinions and egos, it was a very helpful resource. Many cabin building kits were available for self build or finished structures. Options included temporary buildings and tiny homes. This had potential as an option for us, would require less construction knowledge, would come complete with all materials, and be simpler to build. I had found a website that built log structures. Not a fully traditional style log cabin, but machined timbers that slotted together. The four to six inch thick walls, in many styles and designs, ranged from 100 sq feet to 2000 sq feet. The prices started at $10,000 going upwards. This could be the solution we'd been looking for. What I really liked when browsing their site was they had floor plans and dimensions for all the models. This helped us with imagining sizes and floor plans that would suit our needs.

From our stays in the trailer, we realized it is possible to live and have everything you need in a tiny footprint. The trailer design was so compact and probably only 120 sq feet yet had a shower room, kitchen area, dinette, and couch, and pull out beds. How big a space would we want? Dave's started our bidding with 900 sq feet, his reasoning that it was a reasonable sized home for resale and improving the value of the property. I had lived in a small apartment before that had two bedrooms, and bathroom, with kitchen, diner and living space, that was less than 600 sq feet, and plenty big enough.

We liked the idea of a loft bedroom, with bathroom, living and kitchen open plan floor area on the main floor, and perhaps rooms for a guest bedroom. Given there would be no need for excessive storage inside the cabin as we had the workshop and plenty of space for storage sheds, etc. this might be possible in the 600-900 sq ft. There were plenty of cabin kits available in this size range. I showed Dave my findings and, being a visual person, he appreciated seeing the floor plans. Bearing in mind at this stage, it was purely hypothetical, as we were not in any position to move forward with a purchase. They might offer financing. Then again, there was a bunkie kit, a tiny cabin with a loft bedroom that was only $10,000-15,000. This was something we could afford without needing to borrow money. We could start by building something small like this to gain experience and practice. Use it for a while, and then once we were in a better financial position, build a bigger home and use the bunkie as a guest suite. I pitched this idea to Dave; it seemed to satisfy our needs of having a more permanent structure than the trailer. We could have a woodstove for heating, would be warmer and have more space than the trailer, but achievable in a shorter time frame. It might just be a solution.

I had a few questions and sent off an email to the EZ log structures website. To my great surprise, within a few minutes, I had a phone call from Stan. It was an Alberta number. He had received our inquiry and could answer our questions. We wanted to see one of these cabins, to see how big it was inside and the quality of the construction. Stan was based in Lloydminster, a six-hour drive on the Saskatchewan border. It would be a long drive just to view a small building. I wasn't sure if it was worth it, but Dave surprised me with his response.

"Why don't we go this Sunday?" he said. Which was two days away.

"Really? Are you sure? It's a long way to go, just for browsing and future potential."

"Why not? OK, yes, it's far, but once we've seen them, we will know if it's an option or not," he decided.

He didn't need to tell me twice; because of the distance we booked a hotel to stay overnight. I suddenly had another idea to make the trip more worthwhile. There was also another cabin kit building company in Edmonton. Knotty Pine Cabins provided custom designs as kits and had a showroom that we could visit to get more ideas. It seemed worthwhile to take a brief detour on our way back to visit those, too.

Chapter Forty: Cabin Research

On the Sunday we were up early and on the road, to go cabin kit viewing. It was impulsive and incredible that from not knowing what we wanted; we were suddenly committing to a huge step forward. For me, what was more surreal was that Dave had suggested it and was the one to decide. It was still just getting ideas, but by taking action, it seemed one step closer to reality.

The drive was long, but for me into an area I had never been before, so interesting and enjoyable. I loved seeing the green rolling fields of wheat and barley not yet ripened, waving in the breeze and drifting by small farming towns.

We met Stan in his yard, where he had a few models constructed. He was unlocking the gate as we pulled up. It was nice to get out of the car and stretch our legs after hours of driving. The first bunkie was a different model to the one we were interested in, but the same square footage. The loft sleeping area was quite small, with a ladder to access. It was rather like a luxury kids' playhouse or summer house. The designers used engineered logs to construct the walls with dovetail joints at the corners. We viewed all three models, each bigger than the previous. But none had the upper loft area that we wanted for a bedroom, and the roofs were of a low pitch of 4/12. Dave, having roofing knowledge and background, had already established we needed at least a 6/12 preferably 8/12 to help with shedding snow in the winter. Roof pitch (or slope) tells you how many inches the roof rises for every 12 inches in depth. For example, a roof pitch of "8/12 pitch" means that the roof drops 8 inches for every 12 inches horizontally from the peak (or ridge). The higher the pitch, the steeper the roof. We also knew that we needed a design that could withstand a typical snow load of 90lb per square foot.

There are tables for each province and area, stating the average snowfall and accumulation over years of data. The term "Snow load" describes the weight of snow per square foot, that may accumulate on the roof over the winter. The steeper the roof, the more chance the snow will slide off and reduce the weight on the roof. We planned to use a metal roof that helps the snow to slide off, with a steep roof pitch of 8/12 so gravity would help dump the snow, as it built up over the winter.

There were cabin kit models with the 8/12 pitch we wanted, but would probably need additional beam support to withstand the 90lbs snow load. The warm, honey coloured wood interior, and cute windows with alpine style shutters would look perfectly at home in the trees at Fernhaven. The red roofed veranda cried out for a couple of deck chairs to watch the sunset. While inside the citrus pine aroma, was just waiting for a cast iron wood stove crackling with logs burning in the corner. Kettle singing on top. We discussed options with Stan over dinner and explained our idea of starting small and purchasing a second larger model later on. His advice was to not bother with the smaller bunkie but to just build once with a bigger model. We left him with our heads full of ideas and potential. Now we were a step closer to construction sooner than we had thought. We needed to pick the model and get a price for the kit, delivery, and erection from him. Ensuring the cabin could support the snow load was also a requirement.

We still had our second stop at Knotty Pine, to add more information and ideas to the table. Navigating into Edmonton, we arrived at a very industrial area of the city, dumpsters, rail yards, and shabby storage units. Not where we expected to find cute Hansel and Gretel style cabins in the woods. Parking up at the address that our GPS told us we had arrived, a mangy cat wandered through the weeds and disappeared under a chain-link fence. Beyond the fence was a beautiful chocolate box cabin with a peaked green metal roof, large framed windows and knotty pine siding.

"There is no way we can afford something like that" I had already decided, there was no way it was in our budget.

"Well, let's see what they have to say," Dave reasoned. "I'm sure they have different sizes and options."

We found our way into the office and received a spectacular tour of the manufacturing area, show home, and warehouse. It was very impressive. The salesperson had a quick quote system that showed us sizes, finishes, windows, and staircases. I was slightly embarrassed as she asked what our budget was for the build, while we waited for the quote to roll out of the printer.

"Well, we are not sure yet what we can afford," I sidestepped. I wanted to see how much the quote was before offering an amount, not having any idea how much they would be.

At that point, we really didn't know what we could afford, if we could get any more money and if we wanted to. This was more an exercise in fact finding and gathering information, not getting our cheque book out. Also, they were booking for next spring. If we wanted to build next year, we would have to decide within the next month.

The quote for a modest 24 foot x 36 foot cabin was around $100,000, for the kit not including interior finish or construction of the kit. This seemed reasonable for what it included, but we'd have to run the numbers to see if this was a possibility for us.

The five-hour drive home from Edmonton gave us plenty of time to think. We did this mostly in silence, both of us quite overwhelmed by the avalanche of information and needed time to digest everything we had learned.

Both options had pros and cons. EZ Log Structures would for sure be much more economical, but required more sweat equity on our part and a lot more involvement with construction. Knotty Pine offered a much nicer finished end product, but would be a lot more investment.

It felt like our next steps would be to see what the bank had to say. After all, there was no harm in asking to see what they would lend us and how much we wanted to pay out.

I with little thought on the outcome had come around to thinking that to realize the full potential and enjoyment of the land, we must build the cabin sooner. The only way to do that would be to borrow money. I wanted to enjoy the next few years with Dave at Fernhaven. Doing the things we loved, gardening, walking trails, sitting in the sun, having a beer, watching the sunset, in our little haven in the woods. To get to this point, it would be best to get the cabin built sooner rather than later, and getting that part completed so we could enjoy the next stage. We didn't want to drag out construction for over three or four years. By then, who knows what life changes may have happened? The time was right to move forward now.

Chapter Forty-One: Utilities

With the sun beating down, I couldn't imagine we had been shivering with hot water bottles and blankets only a few months before. We had enough water for the garden and trailer tanks thanks to the generator-powered well pump that ran every two hours to pressurize the water line.

Gathering fresh potatoes, swiss chard, and beans for dinner each evening, the fire ban meant we had to cook in the trailer instead of over the open fire. It was too hot for fires and with bright evenings; we didn't miss that fire at all. Vegetables cooked within minutes of being pulled from the ground just taste that much better. We just wished we had more!

The sun was scorching enough to heat water in a small black plastic cistern. I ordered a battery powered shower, which we dropped into the tank and gave us a hot outdoor shower. A refreshing treat after working all day.

After our friends had left, we could finish the trim on the pumphouse and start insulation, looking ahead to colder weather. We inserted polystyrene sheets between the rafter and the pumphouse floor for insulation. We also dug a hole by hand to add a six by six wooden post attached to the side of the pumphouse. This would serve several purposes. First, as a solid anchor for the pumphouse to the ground, provide a secure base for the grounding wires, and act as a mast for the power line from the main line. We would be ready for the electrician to hook us up to the grid. Having power and water were two of our primary goals to not only make life easier, but also to help with future financing.

This time last year we had to bring all our water with us and only had 12 volt power from the trailer battery. We were slowly becoming more self sufficient, with both water and power, but it still took a lot of work to make them accessible. To have power at the trailer required heaving the generator into the cart and pushing it over the rough trail to get it to the summer camp for hookup to the trailer. To get water, we had to take the generator back to the pumphouse. Connect the pump, wait for the line to pressurize and then to switch off the pump before the well ran dry. Then running the hoses to the garden or the trailer. It was closer to convenience, but not like flicking the switch or turning the tap. That would be our goal. We tried not to think of all the hard work that would go into making that possible. If we stopped to think about how much effort that would take, I think it would have been far too daunting to even bother starting.

Now that we had the pumphouse mast installed, we arranged the electrician to install the electrical panel and prepping to hook up to the main line. Then we'd have power, or so we thought.

By the time we got back to Fernhaven in September, the sweltering heat had destroyed the garden. No constant watering resulted in everything wilting and drying up. The beets were small but delicious. But the garden would have to wait. We had a workshop to build.

While most of the work happened when we were at Fernhaven, I was always thinking of things while we were in Canmore. My mind was most definitely focused on being there more and more. It just felt to me like there was so much more opportunity to do things. More space, more garden, more projects, more ideas. Growing up on the farm in the UK, in had been a favourite pastime of my brother and I to build "camps" either in the hay barn, treehouses, or forts in the woods. This felt like a grown-up version of that, looking around to imagine what we could build to make life there more comfortable. Each time we returned to Canmore, I compared our modern, convenient home to what we had in the small trailer. What would make a difference to Fernhaven? Countertop space was one such challenge. It was very minimal in the trailer, and frustrating to have nowhere to chop vegetables, or put dishes, constantly moving things around to make space. What we needed was a solid table that would provide somewhere to prepare food, eat meals, and just space to put things. A picnic bench would be perfect.

Dave and I both visited construction sites to complete safety inspections. Dave is a regular visitor to job sites around Canmore and is well known. Often there is waste lumber that is still usable, even though it may not be good enough for a highly specified building construction. The site superintendants would call us and let us know they had lumber that was going to be discarded and we could help ourselves. We had picked up many loads of 2x4's and 2x6's of various lengths, and currently had quite the stockpile waiting to be transported to Fernhaven, as space would allow. Some of it was too long to take safely in the bed of our truck, but we didn't want to cut it just yet. So we were holding on to it, in case we found a use or way to get it to Fernhaven.

Being thrifty and with time to spare until our next trip, I thought I could build a sturdy picnic bench just like the ones we used at campsites. For a fraction of the cost of buying one, with the lumber we had and the purchase of a few carriage bolts to secure it together. I printed a simple woodwork plan from the internet, and with a spare weekend we got to work. We would partially build the table in Canmore and finish construction at Fernhaven. Selecting suitable pieces was challenging, but we found enough straight pieces. Then slowly measured, cut lengths and drilled out the holes we needed. We finished up with the 8 foot long table top, the two A frame support ends, and all the bench planks ready to piece together on site. Everything sanded down nicely. I couldn't wait to put it together. This would definitely be on the list to be transported on our next trip.

Chapter Forty-Two: Workshop

Once we started construction on the workshop, we knew it would need to be completed before we could leave. When complete, it is a very strong, weather proof structure. During construction, before all the bolts and fasteners are in place and tight, it might collapse or buckle. We had arranged a team of three others to help with the erection. Blake, Rick, and Blake's stepson. They were due to arrive first thing in the morning before the heat of the day.

Eager to be as prepared as possible, we worked into the evening, even though we had driven from Canmore the same day.

The workshop contained 12 metal arches. To assemble the workshop, one must loosely bolt together the seven pieces of each of the arches on the ground. We would then stand each arch up by pulling with a rope and bolt subsequent arches together one by one.

Dave and I positioned the first arch pieces on the concrete and lined up the bolt holes. The galvanized metal, although thin, was heavy and wobbly, and the shape of the pieces made it hard to line up the 50 bolt holes in each arch. We got three arches built before the light was fading too much to continue.

The crew arrived bright and early; it was so exciting to think we could finally put the workshop construction behind us. Dave and I went to pick up some scaffold from our neighbours to help us access the top of the arches. By the time we had returned, Blake and Ryan had the first arch up, using the excavator bucket to stabilize it. Maybe we'd have the whole thing done in a couple of days! With the scaffold built, we attached the ropes and pulled up the second arch. With it swaying precariously halfway up, it was difficult to line up the base of the two arches and needed some serious levering and brute force to get it in place. Each arch weighed about 400lbs, and the top of the arch sagged slightly, resulting in none of the holes lining up with the first arch. We had purchased a tool to push through the two holes to pull them together, but had not expected the effort this would take. Of course, with the tool through the bolt hole, it was not possible to get a bolt through that same hole. We had to wiggle and persuade the metal arches to slide, so the next hole lined up for a bolt. On the straight sections, this worked well, but became more challenging on the curved sections. Two hours later, we had the two arches loosely bolted together. Now to add some bracing inside and outside the building to stop it from warping. It was very slow going. As the minutes ticked by, the temperature soared. Struggling with each bolt hole, with the scorching sun beating down was getting unbearable. By the time we had three arches up, the guys had had enough and retired for the day, promising to be back first thing in the relative cool of the morning.

Dave and I struggled on in the heat to get a couple more arches constructed on the ground. It was as much as we could do before needing a cool dip at the lake.

It was our plan to get more ready in the morning as the guys were pulling up and bolting the next arches. But we also needed to secure the erected arches to the foundation. This required drilling six-inch deep holes into the concrete and was a laborious, noisy, and dusty task. Rick volunteered for first shift and got to work on the hammer drill pounding into the concrete.

The more arches we pulled up, the harder it was getting to line up and attach them together. By the time we had two more arches up, it was too hot again to work, hitting 35C in the sun. The guys had had enough. Day two over and we had five arches up, and two secured with Hilti bolts to the concrete.

Monday, the heat was taking its toll and only Rick showed up. We later heard they had taken Blake into hospital. It was unclear what had happened, but maybe dehydration and heat stroke. Rick stoically pushed on with drilling holes in the concrete. There was little else we could do except get more arches together on the ground.

Not expecting Blake to be back, we were panicking four days in and we had only five arches up, not even halfway. Then we got a text from the general store. There was a guy in there looking for work. He was living up on the mountain and needed some cash. Dave and I debated would we risk giving him a chance? We knew nothing about him. Was he trustworthy? A hard worker? Did we have a choice? He had a phone, but no money for gas for his truck, so we'd have to pick him up. Could he bring his two dogs because he couldn't leave them up on the mountain on their own? It seemed kind of wacky, and not your everyday occurrence, but we needed help. Dave drove down to the store to pick up Tim and his two dogs in the truck.

It turned out to be an excellent decision. Tim was polite and hardworking. By the end of the day, we had another three arches up. Eight done four to go. Rick was unavailable the next day. So no point in getting Tim there, as we needed at least four people to lift the arches.

Dave and I between us could at least get all the arches put together on the ground. Two more days and between us, we finally got all the 12 arches pulled up and loosely bolted together. The concrete drilling had proved too much for Dave's hammer drill. We needed something else. We'd have to take the time to drive in to Vernon to rent a more powerful drill. This would also give us a chance to purchase the cement we needed to seal and weatherproof the bottom of the arches.

Oh boy, did that make a difference? The rented drill powered into the concrete like it was butter. We should have done that from the beginning! So much quicker and easier. By now we were working on pure adrenaline, just doing what needed to be done to get this darn workshop up. I wish I'd never even thought of buying it. Never would we have imagined it would be such hard work. With all the Hilti bolts securely fastened into the concrete, another step was complete. At least it wouldn't blow away in the wind now.

Chapter Forty-Three: Finishing Up

It was wonderful to know we had all the arches up and it looked fantastic. But we still had to tighten all the thousands of bolts. This required one person being on top of the workshop roof holding the bolt while another person inside tightened the nuts.

Dave, who had been a mountain climber most of his life, was more comfortable with heights, so he went on the roof.

Initially, we were unsure how rigid and strong the building was; it had seemed so rickety when raising the arches. Would it hold Dave's weight? Of course, we reasoned it must be able to. If it didn't, then we were in trouble. They designed it for 95lb per square foot snow load. When he first cautiously clambered up, I was fearfully watching on, just waiting to jump in if anything moved. It was completely solid, our worries unfounded. From inside using the baker scaffold, I had the job of supporting the heavy impact driver up above my head to tighten nut after nut. Then clambering down the scaffold, moving it over a few feet and climbing back up, tightening more than back up and down, repeatedly. Towards the end of the day, I could hardly raise my arms at all. I hoped they would have recovered to do it all again the next day.

It was very satisfying as we tightened each bolt to feel the sheets of metal pull together, improving the structural stability with every bolt. Dave, while not having the heavy work I had had, was working on the hot tin roof in the sweltering sun for most of the day. We were very relieved to have the bolt tightening over. We estimated we had gone over each of the 1000s of bolts and nuts multiple times while constructing arches and securing them in place.

With this stage over, we still could not relax and rest yet. Once we had the wooden bracing removed from inside the new shop, it looked quite professional, a shiny new workshop, all the rows of bolts straight and tight.

It was very satisfying to step back and look at the building as an entire structure. The internal space of 20 feet by 24 feet gave adequate space for a shop. Dave suggested we should turn it into a livable area. I think he was joking.

On our trip back from Vernon to return the rented Hilti drill, the electrician called. He was double booked and couldn't come on the day he had scheduled. Would we mind if he re-scheduled? Yes, we minded! It was the last day of our time at Fernhaven and it was vital to have the electrical panel and wiring installed so BC Hydro could come and hook in to the main power line. Dave took over the negotiation. He was very good at maintaining calm and assertive discussions like this. Me? I would just have blown up, got emotional and angry with the guy.

Dave explained our timelines, and it was imperative they come out on the arranged day, and it worked. They rearranged to complete our work.

Our pumphouse now looked much more substantial and official, with an electrical panel and mast. We still couldn't access power yet, but it was another step closer.

There was still a last step for this project that we thought would not be so bad after all the work we'd done so far. We needed to cement in the Hilti bolts and level off the keyway that had given us so much trouble back during the concrete pour. To add structural strength and ensure water running off the roof would drain away from the building instead of running inside.

We borrowed Blake's concrete mixer, and had thought he could get us some sand to mix the cement. Once again, a simple part of the plan turned out to be the most physically hard. He didn't have access to any suitable sand. But he knew of a nearby sand pit we could go get a few loads from. Great! The only downside was we would need to shovel it by hand, into the truck and out of the truck. We had a few tote bins and buckets around the place used to carry tools, etc. so we would head up to the pit, fill them and be back.

We bumped up the forestry road to the pit, both using shovels to fill the buckets and bins. Being careful not to overfill them so we could lift them the 3 feet up into the bed of the truck. Sand bins are heavy. Even though the key way looked small, we had calculated we would need several hundred kilograms of sand to make enough cement.

Blake stayed around to mix up the cement but didn't have long, so it was a race to fill the bins, haul the sand and get it all back to Fernhaven. Blake was mixing, Dave was wheel barrowing, and I was levelling the cement in place at the base of the arches, both inside and outside the building. Smoothing off the cement to give a small gradient on the outside for water to run away from the building. Crouching down in the dusty dirt working the cement, I couldn't wait for it to be finished. It was almost an anticlimax as I troweled the last section smooth. I could at last stand, sore back protesting as I straightened up. We had done it! The workshop was up, secure, and looked amazing. All ready to park the trailer in come winter. We would not have to worry about the trailer being outside this year, and had a dry place to store building materials and tools. We hadn't finished the shop yet, but we could cover the ends with a tarp for temporary protection this year. I parked Bob in the shop just to see how it looked. Just in time for our first rainstorm of the summer. That is a sound I will not forget in a hurry. Standing inside the shop, hearing the rain pattering on the tin roof, being dry and knowing our hard work and sweat had made it happen.

We were due to head home the next day, but took an extra day to enjoy being there without a heavy workload. To rest. We put together and stained the picnic bench. This was such a breeze compared to constructing the shop. We were working on the ground; the parts were simple to lift. All it took was tightening a few bolts, and we had a sturdy picnic bench worthy of the best campsites. We christened it with lunch and a bottle of wine. Sitting with the sun on our backs, albeit sore backs, happy and contented with our progress.

Now we had three permanent structures: the outhouse, the pumphouse, and the workshop. Almost a year to the day since we had completed the purchase of the property. I felt very lucky to challenge ourselves in this way. Few people have the chance to take a raw piece of land and build everything. To know that it has all come from your own imagination, creativity, and hard work.

Chapter Forty-Four: Thanksgiving

Thanksgiving is one of my favourite long weekends. This was our second one at Fernhaven. Last year, we had been building the outhouse. It was wonderful to appreciate and take notice of what we had achieved this year.

Our first task was to inspect the pumphouse BC Hydro had been here in between our visits and finally hooked us up to the power grid. We had electrical power! Well, in theory, we did. There was a brand new shiny cable running from the power line to our pumphouse and a digital meter on the outside, but we had no outlets installed yet. It was enticing to know it was right there, yet unavailable. We still had to start the generator every time we wanted to pump water. The water in the well was gradually dropping, and the pump would run for only a few minutes before it ran dry, but it was enough to water the garden and for our use.

Longer term, we had to come up with a better water set up. Over a 24-hour period, we calculated the well produced plenty of water for what we would need. By adding in additional storage cistern and having the well permanently connected to power, there would be enough water. We could gradually top up the water for larger uses such as a bath or washer. I looked into controllers to turn off the pump automatically when the well was empty, but it seemed another type of pump was necessary. This would be a project for next year, as we planned to disconnect and drain down the system over the winter to prevent frost damage. Once we had access to the power, we could heat the pumphouse to protect the pumps and pipework from freezing. To increase efficiency, we insulated the walls and roof of the pumphouse with rigid polystyrene insulation sheets.

Each day dawned with brilliant blue sky and a nip in the early morning air, but not enough to dip below freezing yet. We enjoyed a blazing fire each night with the fire ban lifted, using it to cook steaks and for warmth. The flames danced and crackled, sending sparks into the air. When I looked up, I could see millions of stars. The more you look, the more seem to appear in layers and layers, then a shooting star, would flash across the sky, disappearing as quickly as it had appeared.

We had been longing to take an exploratory trip up on some new forestry roads to the west. The back roads map we had were perfect for basic navigation but didn't have enough detail to be exactly sure where to go. The bumpy switch backs snaked back and forth as we climbed high above the valley. We couldn't tell how far we'd gone in the thick trees until we broke out of the dense evergreens. From there, we glimpsed the road and our property in the far off haze. It was possible to identify at least four lakes from up there and get a much better sense of the lay of the land. I bookmarked it as the perfect location to bring guests to show them the area. In the far distance, white peaks marked the highest mountains with a dusting of snow, predicting winter to come. But not today. In the sunshine, it was still warm enough to be in t-shirts.

With time to spare, I was keen to get more experience with the Bob cat mini excavator. We had got done what we needed so far. Removed a few stumps, levelled some ground, but for more detailed work and finishing, we still relied on shovels and rakes. I still didn't have the fine motor skills to control the bucket with the joysticks. It took me time to think which joystick to move and which direction to push it to get the bucket angled and moving in the right direction. Our investment in the machine would only be beneficial with time and practice. So far, we probably would have been better paying someone to bring their own equipment and do the work we needed.

There were still piles of earth and rocks, displaced when building the workshop, that we wanted to push into the ditch between the shop and the pumphouse. Filling in the ditch would level up the trail and make it easier to bring the generator between the two locations. It was slow going without a trailer or means to transport the material and required repositioning the excavator many times. Scooping up bucketful's moving them as far as the boom would swing, and dumping in a new pile closer to the end point. By piggy backing the piles, I could move all the material to the ditch. Moving back and forth, using the tracks and blade to level up across the ditch. I was making good progress, having extended the trail about three quarters of the way across the ditch. Before it became clear, we did not have enough left over material to fill the depression completely. I would need to push more material over to at least fill the deepest part of the ditch and reduce the overall steepness. Moving the excavator over the rough soil and rocks I'd moved so far, Bob suddenly began hissing. Plumes of fine mist billowed out from underneath the main body. I immediately powered down, wondering what had happened. Was it steam? No, I realized it was hydraulic oil escaping from somewhere. A hydraulic hose had sprung a leak. It was difficult to see where the oil was coming from, somewhere deep within the hydraulic system underneath the machine. This stopped our work for the day. We placed a request in to the mechanic to ask if he was available to come fix Bob.

A few hours later, Martin had dismantled Bob and left his internal parts strewn all over the driveway like steaming guts. It had not been an easy hose to locate and fix, requiring the seat, and various internal parts removed to access the hose connectors.

There was a company in Lumby who could build us a new hose, while we waited. This was ideal, as we needed a few other supplies for the trailer and the pumphouse. We were discovering, even though remote, there were options and solutions to get what we needed. It seemed our days never ended doing the tasks we had expected to be doing. Excavator operation over for the day, the ditch levelling would have to wait.

Even though the days were still warm, we wanted to get the trailer winterized in readiness for colder weather. Last year had been a hurried affair for winterizing. This year we were determined to complete the exercise properly, and not add antifreeze to the fresh water tank. To do this, we needed to disconnect the water pump in the trailer and pump antifreeze directly from the jug through the pipes. With the extra pipe fitting purchased in Lumby, we could perform this task easily using far less antifreeze and keeping the water tank clean.

After putting Bob back together, I didn't want to do any more excavator work. So, we parked up Bob for the season in the shop. Tying up large tarps at each of the open ends of the shop to keep out rain and snow over the winter. This was only a temporary solution, we hoped, would be substantial enough to withstand any winter storm that might blow through. With several months of winter ahead, we didn't know how the tarps would fare.

Chapter Forty-Five: Searching for Gold

With all the primary goals for the year completed, we had one last adventure planned. Dave had borrowed some gold panning equipment from a friend of his and it had sat redundantly under the trailer all summer. Somehow, we always had more pressing tasks to get done. It had seemed extravagant to waste time and energy searching for the gold claim we had so much to do. Finally, the conditions were right; the weather had cooled a little; the shop was complete, and the snow was long gone from the forestry roads.

From our previous attempt, we were better prepared, with ropes in case the descent was steep, hiking boots, gold pans, and bear spray. Kevin and Ann had warned us the Barnes Creek area had plenty of bears, mainly black bears, but they had spotted the odd grizzly too. I was nervous, remembering looking down into the steep darkness crowded with trees standing and fallen, it had not looked very inviting. Ominous and hiding, who knew what dangers.

I knew how keen Dave was to explore; I was determined to be brave and see it through.

"Do you think we should take the gun with us?" I asked. "Kevin advised us to take it, just in case."

"No, it will be too heavy and difficult to get through the trees with it on my back."

"Well, I'm carrying the bear spray then, its so dark in the trees, we won't see a bear until it's right on us."

I could see his point about the gun, but was still worried about the trek down to the creek.

We spent around 25 minutes to reach the spot where we had to turn back last time. I spied the orange flagging tape we'd marked the beginning of our claim. It was a 50 acre square parcel of land, with Barnes Creek running through the middle. The forestry road ran parallel to the creek. From Google Earth we had assessed it was about half a kilometre from the road to the creek. But what Google Earth could not display was that half a kilometre was a very steep gradient, densely packed with tall cedars, pines, and Douglas firs. Looking down into the darkness, I wondered how some of them were staying upright, clinging to the almost vertical slope. There were many that had failed and lay scattered criss-crossing each other in jumbled piles. How would we find a way through?

Dave surveyed the edge, looking for a lesser slope to start our descent. I geared up with rope, gloves, and back pack carrying the gold pans, sieves, and collection bottles. We were at least optimistic we would get to the river.

"This looks the best spot,"

"OK, let's go," I said, sounding much more brave than I felt.

We cautiously picked our way through a leg breaking pile of deadfall. It was slow going. Once through the fallen trees, the slope continued to drop steeply, our boots sinking into years' worth of spongy pine needles. The only way to navigate safely was to place our boots sideways against the slope and switch back and forth across the soft ground. Dave headed for a patch of sunshine that had miraculously found its way to the forest floor. The rays of friendly sunlight drew us, preferring this to the surrounding dim gloom. It was early afternoon. I couldn't imagine what it would feel like when evening fell. I hoped we would be safe back at Fernhaven by then.

The ground levelled out a little, and I looked back to fix the last glimpse of the truck firmly in my mind. I was looking forward to seeing it again. When we dropped over the next bench, I saw large moss-covered boulders the size of the truck littered across the slope and wondered how long they had been there. Some jammed up against trees and others jumbled together. Had they tumbled down from the mountain before most of these trees had even been saplings?

We made our way farther and farther down, but often forced to traverse left and right to avoid drop offs and near vertical sections. Dave regularly tied some flagging tape to trees so we could find our way back up. They had never logged this section because of the steep terrain, and the trees towered hundreds of feet above us.

As we crested another small bench, the faint rush of water got louder and louder. There was no way to see it through the thick trees, but it was closer. I was constantly looking around for signs of bears and making noise to let them know we were there. But we had seen no signs of any wildlife at all. It was eerily quiet, no birds, chatter of squirrels, or any noise except the increasing roar of the water.

It was getting so loud I kept expecting to see the creek with every step. We moved right to navigate around a large boulder, and squeezed down between the rocks, only to realize the way forward was no longer a steep slope but a sheer cliff. My heart was pounding. I had no head for heights, and looking down over the 15 feet drop, I felt giddy. But at least we could see the river, white water rushing over the rocks below.

That was it. As far as I was concerned, we couldn't get down that we'd found the river. Now it was time to head back up.

"Well, that's that then. Dave, you know how I feel about heights. We can't climb down there. It's far too dangerous. Dave? Please?"

"I think I see a way down."

He pointed over to the right where the cliff petered out into the slope. Sidestepping down, we could creep along the base of the cliff. It was a narrow ledge, with another drop below. I just couldn't see myself being able to make it. My imagination running wild, seeing myself or Dave slip to the rocks below and get washed away down the river. Or Dave being knocked out and me having to leave him to go get help. What if a bear came along while I was gone, finding Dave an easy meal?

"No way, Dave, it's not safe. One of us will fall. It's not worth it."

"I'll go first and take the rope. I can tie it at both ends so you can use it to hold on to. Go slow. It will be fine. Louise, you can do this."

I wasn't so sure about that, but taking the rope he was already halfway across. I couldn't watch as he edged along the narrow ledge, unaware of the jagged rocks below. Safely over, he tied off the rope and beckoned me over. I shakily put one foot out feeling along the ledge, which seemed to slip away from my boot, as I shifted my weight to place my other foot. With the rope securely wrapped around my hand to be sure I couldn't let go, if I fell, with Dave coaching me where to place my feet, at last I was across. Dave enthusiastically hi-fived.

"You did it!"

We were down. The river in a narrow gorge disappeared over a foaming white water mass of rocks down stream. There were a couple of spots with gravel interspersed between the boulders, where we could reach the water. It seemed probable given the difficult access that no one had been to this section of the creek before. Maybe it would be the ideal spot for gold. After the scary descent, it was nice to sit and relax on a rock in the sun for a few minutes. Dave got out the pans and small shovel from the backpack. We looked around, wondering what to do. The thing was, neither of us knew anything about gold panning. We had read a couple of books from the library and watched a few YouTube videos. It had looked a lot easier than it felt now we were here at the river bed.

We loosened up the gravel on the small beach area and dumped it into the pan. Dipping into the water and swirling it around to wash over the lighter sediment and rocks. Picking out larger rocks, until all we had left was a small crescent of water, dark sandy material balanced in the corner of the circular pan. Not really sure what we were looking for. I spotted a small shiny speck and showed it to Dave. It was quartz and mica. No gold so far.

After the trek down, it was quite a back strain to bend over the water, swishing and swirling pans full of sand and gravel. Exciting and fun to wonder what might be there. But also worrying, wondering if we were actually washing away any tiny flakes of gold, because of poor technique. It would have been ideal if we had someone to show us good spots, or demonstrate the correct technique for panning. After a couple of hours, we still had found nothing. Not sure if it was our method or there really was nothing there. I suspect it was our lack of experience. It was fun and we could now at least say we had been panning on our gold claim. We called it a day, as the afternoon drew on. The sun disappeared from the canyon, and I wanted to be back in the truck before it got any darker.

It was much easier going back up. Not having to look down the steep slope, but up towards the light. Finding the flagging tape we had used to mark the trail proved more difficult than you would think. We had imagined we came straight down, but had, in fact, followed quite a winding path in navigating obstacles. Finally, I could see the white body of the truck, our escape, the sun glinting off the paint work high above us. I think I almost ran the last section in relief to be back on the forestry road.

We won't forget the adventure despite the challenges, but it disappointed us not to find a big nugget. However, we didn't find it surprising. Perhaps we will come back and try our luck again.

Chapter Forty-Six: Security

There were always small ideas popping out of my head, random but usually rooted with a need we identified. As we developed more and more infrastructure and added value to the land, security while we were away was an ongoing concern.

We had heard of thefts in the area, and wanted to add another level of security. We did not want to fence in the entire five acres, thinking it better for wildlife to allow them to roam freely and not get hindered by barriers. If we posted certain signs prohibiting trespass, they considered the land in BC being enclosed, even with no fences. This we had done. But it was still far too easy for a vehicle to drive in, and they may argue that they did not know it was private land.

I'd been hunting for some gates for a while, but they were too expensive, the wrong size or too far away to make it economic to collect them. Not to be deterred, we had plenty of wood; I decided we could make some simple gates of exactly the right size. Which would make it impossible for a trespasser to claim they didn't know it was private land. It would not stop the determined thieves, but would be a minor deterrent. My lack of skill made it hard to dig a posthole with

Bob the excavator, but the sandy soil at the gate spot was easy to dig by hand. We were getting good at digging holes! An hour later, we were straightening and levelling the posts and tamping in the concrete we'd mixed up in the wheelbarrow. After securing the post hinges and hanging the gates, Dave stood back to admire our work. It felt nice to swing the gates shut as we left, giving a visual sense of security, even if that's all it was.

Chapter Forty-Seven: Cabin Fever

Since visiting the cabin kit companies back in the summer, our decision-making process had slowly moved forward. We had researched the yurt option and discovered it was not the simple or economic choice we had imagined. When adding in the foundation, insulation, and add-ons required for snow load, it would be about the same price as a cabin. Many had issues with condensation in yurts in colder temperatures, so it was another reason we were not keen, given BC's damp climate. A more traditional cabin style home appealed to us and after visiting the cabin and kits, we were excited by the potential.

Inquiring about financing for the cabin while renewing our mortgage with the credit union was opportune. Late-night conversations between Dave and I had been productive, well, kind of. Dave had agreed we would find out what it would cost to build, find out if we could borrow that amount, and find out if we could afford to repay it. A lot of 'ifs' but at least we were considering options.

The credit union news was positive, and the numbers looked good. The amount we could borrow was realistic and affordable. We knew our work so far had increased the value of the land, so with a favourable appraisal, it was looking like we could move forward to planning a cabin.

I was excited, but wanted us to be sure to explore all options before we committed to purchasing a cabin kit. Yes, the kits were a good option for beginner builders. Yes, they would simplify the build. But we would still need to prepare the foundation, still need to build the kit, still need to finish the interior. There were still a lot of stages of construction, even with a kit. I had more questions. What would it cost to build a similar size cabin if we did everything ourselves?

This led to a more primary question: what size cabin did we want? It's easy when looking at plans to get carried away. What space do we really need? A bedroom, a bathroom, a kitchen/living area. If possible, room for guests to come stay. How much square footage does a bathroom need? If this was just a summer vacation home, we would be outside often. I wanted an outdoor kitchen and a covered deck. We had the shop for storage. Given a blank canvas about planning a dream cabin, it was difficult to know where to start. Neither of us being very creative and imaginative in designing the cabin floor plan. Lots of questions and possibilities. We used the cabin floor kits as a starting point to help us dial in to what was important to us. I wanted it to be a small, compact, cozy cabin. Enough space to live comfortably. Our workshop gave us the perfect visual example of what a 20 x 24 foot print would look like. It seemed plenty big enough, especially if we could add a loft for the bedroom. This gave us our starting point.

We had the idea of size. Now how could we work out what it would cost to build? I began googling "self build cabin plans" ideally looking for a cabin plan, with a material list or take-off. Having this list would give me what I needed to price up materials to find out the cost to build ourselves. After looking at what felt like hundreds of plans, I found one that had plans, a material list and even step-by-step instructions on how to build it! Seemed to be a good starting point and worth a closer look. I am almost ashamed to admit I found it on Etsy!

It was a 16 x 20 cabin, with a 9/12 pitch roof, designed for the snow load we expected, with a loft bedroom. Before I could find more alternatives to agonize over, I bought and downloaded the full set of plans. Even if we didn't end up building this cabin, it was worth the money as part of our research. Dave and I spent a full weekend getting prices from the Home Depot website using the full material list. Using Home Depot as a worst-case scenario, we thought we could get better prices for a large order. So Home Depot would give us a good sign of how much the materials to build a small cabin would cost. To provide a comparison to the price of the cabin kits.

The kit it self only included the wood to build, windows, doors, no foundation, no insulation, and no metal roof. So we were already aware there would be at least another 30-40% on top of the kit cost.

We drew up a costing spreadsheet with everything we could think of. Cement, timber, flooring, foundation, insulation, windows, doors, roofing material, siding, appliances, interior finishing. It was overwhelming to think of everything. The list kept growing and growing. The biggest surprise for us was it would be approximately half the cost of the kit to buy the materials. This gave us a lot to think about. Obviously, a kit given our lack of building experience would most likely be easier to construct. But working with our small budget, we could only afford the kit and still need more cash to finish it. We might have to go much smaller size if we chose a kit. I wasn't keen on running out of money with only the shell built and then struggling to finish the interior.

If we were prepared to build ourselves, we could opt for a bigger cabin and have enough cash to complete everything. It was all a desktop exercise, as we were not sure of what additional financing we could get. Now we had two routes as potentials to build with a kit or build ourselves. To my surprise, Dave was leaning towards constructing the cabin ourselves. His reasoning being that it would be more economic. We could build the size we wanted and have enough money to finish everything. We had to renew our existing mortgage for the purchase of the land, so planned to ask about another stage of financing. With the global economy threatening recession, interest rates had nowhere to go but up. This cost us a 30% hike to our monthly payment for the land, but even with the increase, it was still very affordable. After running the numbers, our account manager was happy to inform us we could get additional financing pending a favourable appraisal.

Chapter Forty-Eight: Snow

It was now early November, and we arranged our last visit to Fernhaven for the year around Remembrance day to take advantage of the extra holiday. It was yet again going to be a busy few days; we needed to move the trailer into the shop, get everything stored away for winter. Drain the well pump and water line to prevent burst water pipes. Last year we had been planning the concrete pour for the workshop at the same time and been very lucky with the weather. This year was a different story.

During the summer, we had spread the huge tarp from the trees over the trailer to provide shade. On our thanksgiving visit, we did not have time to take it down, thinking we had plenty of time to complete that task in November. Well, mother nature had other plans, just to let us know who's in charge. We knew it had snowed from the trail cam images. As we pulled into camp in the late dim November afternoon, we realized how much of an issue this was going to be. Even though it was only about 2 inches of snow, the tarp weighed down by the heavy wet slush had collapsed onto the trailer. Our mosquito gazebo, not really built to withstand the snow, had completely buckled and lay in a jumble heap of bent metal and soggy canopy.

Rather than stress and argue about whose fault it was that we had not taken down the tarp last time, we opted for a more mature approach. (It was Dave's choice to leave the tarp by the way!) They lifted the fire ban! We could enjoy the new firepit. Luckily the wood pile was dry, and we soon had a roaring fire steaming and melting the snow in the bottom of the pit. Bundled in jackets, hats, and gloves, we still felt soothed to be back outside by the warm fire. Back in Canmore, we wouldn't dream of being outside in this weather, but here we are standing around the fire. Our chairs buried under the frozen tarp. Why did it feel so perfect to be here? faces hot from the glowing flames, backs cold from the chill blowing off the snow. Beer can in hand, just enjoying being outside in our little haven, savouring the peace and quiet that only a snow covered landscape can provide.

Our first task of the next morning was to remove the tarp and clear the way to tow out the trailer. We needed to get this done before the frozen ground softened up and we might get stuck. It was harder than we thought. What looked like a simple one inch of snow on the tarp was actually a frozen layer of ice covered in snow and was unbelievably heavy. No amount of heaving and effort could we pull the pooled frozen puddles of ice off the mangled gazebo. We resorted to a pickaxe and shovel to break up the ice and heaved it out in huge chunks until eventually the tarp flopped free of its extra layer. Once we had the area cleared, I reversed the truck in to hitch up. Reversing in through the trees was tricky, but I thought driving out would be simpler. The first section went perfectly to plan, the crisp frozen surface held up well. In four-wheel drive, the truck had no problem pulling the trailer on to the driveway. Then I ran into problems. The trees I had been reluctant to cut down to provide a nice gentle curve to the driveway crowded in, proving an impossible angle to get the trailer through. No amount of shunting back and forth gave me the direction I needed to navigate around the trees. Reversing in, we had plenty of space. In this direction, not a chance. I gave up once I got the trailer snuggly stuck between a tree on one side and the truck on the other. Thank goodness for the chainsaw, sadly it was our only option to remove another tree. Dave consoled me with the fact we have thousands of trees here. My driving skills disappointed me and I felt guilty about cutting down the tree. A tree that had spent many, many years growing on that spot, just because we needed to move our trailer. Once it was down, the trailer move became a lot easier. We pulled it out to the main driveway and then reversed it in towards the workshop. This was a pivotal moment. The primary reason we had built the shop was to house the trailer and protect it over the winter. We were finally a year later than planned, getting to complete the task.

As I reversed the trailer toward the open end of the workshop, it became alarmingly obvious the trailer roof was very close to the roof of the workshop. We had calculated the height over a year ago, and I questioned my calculations. The shop roof peaked at 11 feet but then sloped away on each side to 7 feet at the wall. Did the height of the trailer include the air conditioning unit? The unit in the centre of the trailer sat about 18inches above the trailer roof. It was clear we would need to reverse the trailer dead centre into the shop to have any chance of clearing the air conditioning unit under the shop roof.

The closer the back of the trailer got to the front of the shop, the bigger the trailer seemed to get. There was a slight ramp up to the concrete floor of the shop and as I slowly reversed closer and closer, the trailer roof got closer and closer to the workshop roof. I hoped as the trailer levelled out, the back end would drop a bit. I jumped out to survey what was going on and realized it wouldn't be the air conditioning unit that scraped the shop roof. But it might be the two corners of the trailer roof, where the shop roof slanted away to the walls. Back in the truck, I had to rely on Dave's guidance, as I couldn't see the back of the trailer entering the shop. With inches to spare, we slowly squeezed the trailer into the shop. It sure made the shop look a lot smaller, with the trailer taking up most of the space. But we got it in, with much relief. It did not bear thinking about, if it had not fit. I wouldn't be able to look Dave in the eye, for all the trouble it had caused to build the shop, and then find the trailer didn't fit.

There was even enough space to squeeze Bob the Bobcat alongside the trailer. The view from the trailer window wasn't much to look at, but we felt happy protecting the excavator and trailer from the oncoming winter weather.

Our next task was to drain and winterize the pump house. Once we bury the pipes and heat the pump house, we won't need to drain and winterize it in the future. However, at this point, we need to take precautions. The water line was still above ground, running from the pumphouse to the shop and the pump in the pumphouse full of water. If it froze over the winter, chances were we would have leaks and need to replace the pump. It was easy enough to disconnect and drain the pump, but the water line was over 200 feet long and full of water. A compressor would have been handy, but we didn't have one. Walking along, lifting the pipe worked to a certain extent using gravity to drain the water, but over that distance, it wasn't enough to fully drain the line. We needed air pressure to blow out the water. We had a bicycle pump. When you are out in the middle of nowhere with a problem, you work with the resources you have. By hooking up the bicycle pump to the pumphouse end of the line, and duck taping to ensure no air leaks, with a little manpower, we could build up enough pressure to force out most of the water. It wasn't ideal and didn't clear all the water, but it was the best we could do with what we had. We just hoped no animals would chomp through the water line over the winter, but we'd deal with that if needed next year.

It was dark by 5pm and we needed some supplies, so headed down to Edgewood before the store closed. Dave was driving back to Fernhaven when suddenly a deer jumped out of the ditch. I heard a bump as it hit the front of the truck and looked back to see if we hurt it.

"Dave! Stop! I think it's on the road."

"It jumped out of nowhere. I had no chance to avoid it,"

"Yes, but let's go back and see. We can at least pull it off the road."

Dave reversed back with hazard lights flashing. There in the road was a young female deer, no marks on her, but clearly knocked out and not moving. Another vehicle pulled up to see what had happened.

"She's done for," the guy said. "We need to put her down quickly. It would be the kindest thing."

We didn't have a gun, and neither did they, but they had a knife. He quickly severed the major artery in her neck to bleed out. Now what to do with the carcass? They only had a car and didn't have room to take the deer with them. We weren't set up to butcher and process a whole deer either, but knew our neighbours would be glad of the venison. At least this way it would not go to waste. We loaded the deer into the back of the truck and called our neighbours on the way home to let them know we had fresh venison if they wanted it. Brett began processing and hanging the meat as soon as we dropped it off, despite the night already several degrees below freezing. We felt sad for causing her death, but we found consolation knowing that someone would appreciate and use the meat instead of leaving it at the side of the road. That was not the end of the evening we expected, but we were coming to learn that very often things did not turn out the way we imagined. It was best to just go with the flow.

With our primary tasks of the trip completed, a sense of relief ensued. But we still had 3 days. What could we fit in? Now there was a good covering of snow, and we were safe from the threat of fires. We could begin burning the brush we had been thinning out over the last year.

It reminded me of bonfire night in England. Every year on November 5th, there is a bonfire and fireworks to commemorate the gunpowder plot. The gunpowder plot of 1605, when Guy Fawkes failed to blow up the houses of parliament. We had no Guy Fawkes effigy or fireworks, but we had a large fire to burn the thinned brush around the workshop and camp. Nothing like dragging brush and branches through the snow, and throwing them onto the fire to get the blood pumping and warmed up. We could even thaw and dry out our frozen and damp chairs by holding them close to the fire. Steaming, then slowly warming, they were dry enough to sit in after a few hours. This was the fun I had imagined, no heavy duty construction, but tidying up, cultivating and thinning the trees, to guard against wildfires.

It was getting colder at night. Our trailer had a propane fuelled heater and warmed up quickly with the fan blowing hot air, but was noisy and as soon as it kicked off the cold seeped back in. The trailer is not insulated against any type of cold weather. We were warm enough when sleeping with a hot water bottle to warm the sleeping bags, but didn't want to sit around in the evenings as it was too chilly. In the mornings, using the propane to cook a breakfast of bacon and eggs and warm up the living area. By the time the day of departure rolled around, we had completely cleared and removed all the wildfire fuel and tidied up the area, ready for next year. We felt happy with our progress, having safely tucked away our trailer and Bob in the shop protected from heavy snow.

It was a habit as we turned out onto the main road when leaving to reflect on how we felt about our trip. Had we achieved what we wanted? Were we sad to leave? For me, it was always the same. I felt sad to be leaving, happy with what we had achieved, but so empty, not knowing when we would be back. Fernhaven was an emotional roller coaster that was addictive. Life back in Canmore was comfortable, but somehow lacked the challenge and excitement. I was always thinking about when we would be back, and couldn't bear the thought it might be several months. All the everyday things - money, career, chores - that had been important before, now seemed less so.

Chapter Forty-Nine: That's a Wrap #2

Back home in Canmore on November 13, we were in a reflective mood. We had spent 55 nights in Fernhaven this year, so much more than our 19 nights last year. What had we achieved? We had built the shop, started the garden, created our summer camp, built the pumphouse, pumped water from the well, and hooked up power. Now, instead of an undeveloped forest, we had the start of our homestead. It was becoming more familiar and like home. There was still a lot to do, but we were happy with our first full year of development. We had also made decisions about the next steps. We would, pending finance, begin the cabin build next year. Small progress so far, but big plans.

But there was so much more depth to what we had achieved. As a couple, it had transformed our relationship. Before this project we had been two adults, who just happened to like the same activities, so it made sense to do them together. There was nothing tangible to tie us together, no joint purchase or assets we owned together. We purchased our possessions separately prior to our relationship. We had shared many exciting and challenging experiences; hiking

300km across England on the coast to coast trail. Completing a 7 day backpacking trip on the West Coast Trail in British Columbia. These had been tough, and physically challenging trips, where we had needed to rely on each other for support. Both were amazing trips we'd loved and enjoyed together. But these were bucket list item we had both wanted to do and could have done individually. Finding and buying Fernhaven was a project where we were both committed to the same goal and building something we could share. Both the challenges of developing it and enjoying it once it was complete. We were both committed and responsible for Fernhaven jointly. We didn't always see eye to eye, but we had to work together to solve our problems. It so far had brought us closer together. We both felt more secure in the relationship and were confident we could find solutions, even if we disagreed initially.

Also, it has helped us to understand each other, appreciate and be grateful for what each person brings to the project. Dave is calm, logical, and loves the detail oriented work. He has handled the finance applications, permits, and legalities. He also loves buying tools, power tools, gadgets, generators, chainsaws, scaffolding, etc. All things that we don't even need, but then later I reluctantly come to appreciate having. I am more emotional, creative and jump in on impulse, the dreamer who comes up with the ideas, and Dave helps realize them. I have more hands on experience with construction, using tools, and a research mindset. If I don't know how to do something, I will find out and just get started. I am a problem solver, with determination and tenacity to keep going until it works.

Each of our strengths compliment each other, neither of us could do this project alone, we need each other, in a complimentary way.

We also did not realize how finding Fernhaven was going to change our daily lives so much. We both work as health and safety consultants, which gives us flexibility to pick and choose contracts. It is fulfilling and rewarding work we enjoy. We spend our weekdays on this and then unwind by reading, watching a movie or relaxing in the evenings. We both enjoy exercise and stay fit in the gym exercise classes, biking and hiking. Weekends would see us planning some day hike, biking trip, skiing or snowshoeing in winter. Our primary focus was on working and leisure activities.

Research about building and construction, well water, and servicing the Bobcat take up more time now. Fernhaven is always on our minds. We are either preparing to go to Fernhaven, at Fernhaven or recovering from the physical demands of construction. There is less time for leisure activities and more time spent working on Fernhaven. It's taken over as our full-time project. I really enjoy that new challenge, how it pushes us out of our comfort zone, to become different people. It can be intimidating not knowing what to do, but we power through and it's rewarding in the end. It is changing who we are. What we filled our lives with before felt somewhat superficial and as if we were just filling in time. Now we were working on tangible projects that will outlive us and make a difference to our lives.

If we went for a hike, it is pleasurable exercise and you get to see marvellous views, and create memories that will hopefully last a lifetime. But it really is only a personal gain.

Now we have built the workshop, that is something that will provide shelter and storage and be useful for many years.

It is a solid structure that will be useful for us and others. It is something more than for just one person.

So now it is winter time again, time to make plans and get organized for the next phase. We know we want to build a cabin sooner rather than later. We have decided to finance this instead of save and construct as we go, as this would take longer than we want. Now we have to find out what we can borrow, and work out what we can build with the money we can get. If that all works out, we then have to learn how to build it! Thank goodness we have several months of winter to prepare for the next phase.

Acknowledgements

Thanks to Jenny Palmer for her editing and proof reading work throughout the book, little did you know how much time and work it would be; to my mum Rose Hodges for her encouraging words and ever patient ear in listening to my ideas; to the members of my mums book club in England who kindly offered their time to read the first draft and give me valuable constructive criticism to help improve the story; to my dad John Hodges and step mum Ronnie Hodges for the hours of WhatsApp calls offering encouragement, ideas and moral support in developing Fernhaven; my friends and family who tirelessly and patiently let me ramble on when all I could think about was the land; and finally to my love Dave for enabling my dream to come true, for his quiet calm nature in keeping my feet on the ground, and letting me honestly share our story.

We were in search of a piece of land and did not realize how much more we would gain in the new friends and neighbours we now have, thankyou for your help, lending of tools, time and advice. Our lives are so much richer for knowing you.

Thankyou to every one and all who have listened, offered advice, encouragement, there are too many friends and acquaintances to mention who's influence has made this story.

About the Author

Louise Green believes in pursuing dreams and not making excuses. She grew up on a small farm in England. Leaving her family and a successful career in the UK to pursue adventure in the Canadian Rockies with her 18-month-old son. 20 years later, she has realized her dream of owning a remote piece of land in the forest. Her construction knowledge and skills are self taught. Now a freelance technical writer, she has turned her talent in writing to sharing her journey of transforming the raw forest into a home.

Visit www.LittleHavenintheWoods.com for a photo diary of the project.

Printed in Great Britain
by Amazon

42090506R00121